THE GREAT
CITRUS
BOOK

Allen Susser

Photography by

Lois Ellen Frank

TEN SPEED PRESS

Berkeley, California

*This book is dedicated to my parents Molly &
Paul who enjoy more citrus than anyone I know.*

Copyright © 1997 by Allen Susser

Photography © 1997 by Lois Ellen Frank

Ten Speed Press
P.O. Box 7123
Berkeley, California 94707

Distributed in Australia by Simon & Schuster Australia, in
Canada by Publishers Group West, in New Zealand by
Tandem Press, in South Africa by Real Books in Singapore
and Malaysia by Berkeley Books, and in the United
Kingdom and Europe by Airlift Books.

Text with Frank Flynn

Cover and interior design by Fifth Street Design

Library of Congress Cataloging-in-Publication Data

CIP data on file with the publisher

First printing, 1997

Printed in Hong Kong

2 3 4 5 6 7 8 9 10 — 01 00 99 98 97

Contents

Introduction

Although my culinary education has covered all sorts of fruits, working in depth with citrus has greatly expanded my horizons. I made citrus a staple in my New World cuisine, because it is virtually synonymous with my adopted state of Florida. However, its variety, depth, and substance far surpassed my expectations. I have found the world of citrus to be as fertile, abundant, and enduring as our own recorded history. In many ways, its evolution parallels that of human culture.

The various species of the genus *Citrus* are believed to be native to the subtropical and tropical regions of Asia, although we don't know what that early citrus looked like. But we do know that the fruit has been cultivated for approximately 4,000 years in southern China and Southeast Asia.

Citrus types are separated into different botanical species of the original genus, or scientific classification. These species include the orange (*C. sinensis*), grapefruit (*C. paradisi*), lemon (*C. limon*), lime (*C. aurantifolia* and *C. latifolia*), mandarin orange (*C. reticulata*), and sour orange (*C. aurantium*). Minor citrus species include the pummelo (*C. grandis*), the citron (*C. medica*), and kumquats genus (*Fortunella*).

The range of Citrus is enormous. The hundreds of varieties and subspecies make it the most commonly propagated fruit, cultivated commercially in over 100 countries. Because the yield of the average citrus tree far exceeds that of any deciduous tree (such as apple, pear, peach, or plum), citrus is an economic mainstay for many countries.

The hybridization (crossbreed) process has made citrus one of the most complex fruits on earth. This book will help you discover more exotic species—as well as learn more about the everyday orange.

CITRUS THROUGHOUT HISTORY

Fairest of all God's trees, the orange came and settled here,
Commanded by Him not to move, but grow only in the south
country. . .—Chu Sung

No other fruit has been as well documented or examined as citrus. The word orange derives from the Sanskrit word *naranga* for "orange tree." The Hindus called the orange a *naranga*, which evolved into the Persian word *naranj*. This name was carried throughout the Mediterranean by the Muslims. In Byzantium, the orange was renamed the *nerantzion*, which eventually became *arangium*, *arantium*, and *aurantium*. This mutated into *naranja* in Spain, *laranja* in Portugal, *arancia* in Italy, and *orange* in France, which gave us the modern word.

Citrus fruits are native to southern China and Southeast Asia where they have been cultivated for approximately four thousand years. An advanced stage of the sweet orange was cultivated in China, long before it was introduced to Europe; references to sweet oranges and mandarins are found throughout ancient Chinese literature. The earliest reference was in the "Yu Kung," or "Tribute of Yu," about an emperor who reigned in the years 2297 to 2205 B.C. Ch'u Yuan's first poem "Li Sao" ("Falling into Trouble") mentioned citrus plants and trees of the period around 314 B.C. The "Chu Lu," written in A.D. 1178 by Han Yen Chich, describes twenty citrus varieties.

Citrus traveled the world with traders who brought it to eastern Africa, the Middle East, and southern Europe from Asia. Soon, these countries began cultivating citrus for themselves. Portugal was the first country to cultivate a superior sweet orange in Europe. This single fruit launched the entire citrus industry.

The West, too, has its share of citrus lore. In the Bible, Leviticus 23:40 (ca. 1000-900 B.C.) refers to the "fruit of the goodly tree," or hadar, which is believed to be a citrus. In the Jewish Feast of the Tabernacles, celebrants carry myrtle, willow, and palm boughs to which a citron is attached. Some sects of Judaism consider the citron the apple of the Garden of Eden. The citron is also mentioned in Persian literature (356-323 B.C.) and in European literature of about the same date (310 B.C.) Even the most classic Western stories mention citrus—Hercules retrieves the golden fruit from the Isle of Hesperides as his eleventh major labor.

The popularity of the orange in the Mediterranean seemed only to flourish and as such, so too did the need to protect this fragile fruit. Seneca's nineteenth epistle (ca. 50 B.C.) tells of the Roman use of mica, a transparent mineral that separates into thin leaves to shelter the most delicate plants in their gardens against the cold. Soon, entire structures were designed for this sole purpose. Known as *stanzone per I cidri*, these structures, built about A.D. 81-96, were the earliest greenhouses. In fact, the Europeans later called these buildings *orangeries* in honor of their celebrated occupants.

In 1494, Charles VIII of France originally went to Italy to conquer the peninsula but instead became enthralled by Italian art, lifestyle, and oranges. Charles returned to France with an entourage of Italian craftsmen, gardeners, artists, and architects, determined to transform French castles and gardens in the Italian style. It was at his Chateau d'Amboise that he built the first French orangerie. In the ensuing two centuries, every monarch in every European country built a new orangerie, each larger and more magnificent than its predecessor. Windows reached from floor to ceiling in these buildings, and mica was placed on the windows to seal off the cold—much like today's greenhouses. But no European orangerie was as grand as the one at the Palace of Versailles outside Paris. Built in the shape of a C, this 1,200-foot-long building was a tribute to Louis XIV's love of oranges and orange blossoms.

Citrus arrived in the Americas in 1493 with Columbus' second voyage. The first plantings of sweet orange in what is now the United States occurred between 1513 and 1565 in and near the Florida settlement of St. Augustine, along the St. Johns River. By 1707 reports associated with the spread of the missions in lower California, Sonora Mexico, and Arizona mention oranges.

The lime was first mentioned by Sir Thomas Herbert in 1677, when he referenced a site near the coast of Mozambique. The grapefruit—a probable mutation of the Chinese pummelo—was first described in 1750 by Griffity Hughes, who named it the '"forbidden fruit." Near the end of the eighteenth century, oranges, lemons, and limes were planted throughout Australia and sweet oranges were planted in Hawaii.

Mandarin oranges from southern China did not arrive in Europe and the Americas until the nineteenth century, but were later cultivated to perfection in Malta, Sicily, and throughout southern Italy.

In 1822, Florida became a territory of the United States, and a citrus industry quickly developed. St. Augustine groves began producing nearly three million oranges a year. Two particularly notable Florida groves, the Mays Grove at Orange Mills on the St. Johns River and the Dummitt Grove on Merritt Island, made the Indian River region famous for its production of premium quality fruit.

Grapefruits were introduced to Florida in 1823 by Count Odette Phillipe who came to Safety Harbor (now known as Tampa Bay). Florida started again to export to the northeastern market in 1885 by promoting grapefruit as a novel and exotic fruit. Soon, grapefruit became a staple for breakfast from Charleston to Boston, cut in half to be eaten with a spoon or squeezed fresh for juice.

Although it was only in 1834 that citrus was planted outside a mission in California, the 1860s saw a proliferation of citrus in California. Tulare County was seeded with citrus trees and became the most important citrus growing belt in the state. Small citrus orchards began to spring up and thrive, establishing California's citrus economy. In 1873 Eliza Tibbets planted the most famous orange—the Washington Navel—at her doorstep in Riverside, California, and so started an agricultural phenomenon.

Gold diggers in Northern California sought out oranges from Los Angeles and San Diego until planting began in the San Francisco and Sacramento areas. The first citrus of Northern California, planted by Judge Joseph Lewis in 1856, survives today as the "Mother Orange." It is the oldest and largest living orange tree in California.

By 1875 transcontinental railroads brought California citrus to Eastern markets, and actual sales began in 1877. In 1892 California began shipping citrus to Europe and opened the international market for the California product.

Citrus in the Modern Age

Citrus as food, medicine, ornaments, and cosmetics has now made a great circle from old to new worlds, and from East to West and back. It has traveled the length and breadth of the earth, and its story links every country it has touched and from whose soil it has grown. Today a wide range of citrus varieties are available for commercial and home gardening. Citrus is grown in tropical and subtropical climates throughout the world where there is suitable soil, sufficient moisture, and a decided lack of frost. Still, the vigor, growth, quality, and quantity of the fruit vary greatly according to climate.

The Citrus Belt

Citrus is produced in regions that occupy a "belt" around the world, following the equator and extending approximately 35 degrees latitude to the north and south. Many commercial citrus products are restricted to the subtropics, located between 20 and 40 degrees north and south of the equator. Productivity is greatest in areas with seasonal changes. In areas closest to the equator where warm temperatures prevail throughout the year, citrus is grown largely for local consumption. The warm temperatures in the Tropics speed growth and maturation of the fruit and result in a very short harvest period. Citrus from the tropics accounts for only about 10 percent of world production

Brazil and the United States lead the world in citrus production. Together they produce 42 percent of the world's citrus crop (most of which is processed rather than eaten fresh). The growing conditions of these areas fall between those of the tropical and subtropical climates.

In the colder subtropical regions, orchards need to be heated to lessen frost damage. Although oranges can thrive despite occasional light frost, a hard frost of long duration will kill the trees. Such an event wiped out Florida citrus groves in 1895 and has periodically threatened U.S. crops since.

Propagation and Cultivation

Propagation of citrus trees involves grafting the desired variety to a specific type of rootstock. Growers prefer budded trees over seedlings as they are reliably true to type. They produce fruit sooner, have a greater tolerance to cold and resistance to disease, have a higher quality of fruit, mature earlier, adapt better to adverse soil conditions, and can be dwarfed.

To prepare a fertile growing environment for the trees, the ground is fertilized and a *cover crop* is harrowed into the soil. Citrus trees usually bear fruit four to six years after the initial planting and some will survive for almost a century more. Harvesting is generally done by hand, although a mechanical process of harvesting fruit for juice is being pioneered in Florida.

Most commercial orchards today grow composite trees, whose rootstocks differ genetically from their tops, or scions. Rootstocks are selected by their ability to tolerate various pests, diseases, or adverse soil conditions, while the scion is chosen for its superior fruit quality. The scion is then grafted onto a compatible rootstock, which usually is a citrus of entirely different variety. Although combinations vary, sophisticated production systems have been developed for most citrus types.

Many citrus growers sell their produce through cooperative packing and marketing associations, while others sell to large corporations. Packing centers box the fruit to be sold whole or send it on to processing plants. Oranges picked for use as fresh fruit may be exposed to ethylene gas to bring out the orange color.

Insect Management

Citrus groves are highly susceptible to insects and fungus, and to prevent loss or damage, a grower may choose to use an appropriate legal insecticide or fungicide. Newer chemicals are more environmentally sound and have lowered the toxicity of chemically sprayed fruit while still controlling insects and fungus. Some growers use natural predators to control pests instead.

Citrus Use and World Production

In 1944 scientists found a way to concentrate the juice in a vacuum and freeze it without destroying the flavor or vitamin content and revolutionized the citrus industry. Soon frozen juice was widely available and became very popular. Today about 70 percent of the U.S. orange crop goes to plants for processing. Chilled orange juice, a fresh, nonconcentrated product, is also marketed but at a higher price.

Citrus plays a major role as a raw material for the food industry. Fresh fruit is processed into juice (frozen-concentrated, canned, or refrigerated), canned segments, marmalades, cattle feed (made from the peel), essential oils, pectin, and other chemicals. Oranges account for 65 percent of all citrus production, whereas mandarins (including hybrids such as tangelos and tangors) command about 15 percent; lemons and limes, 10 percent; and grapefruit, 10 percent. The 1995-1996 growing season produced over 64 million tons of citrus worldwide. Brazil produced over 16.5 million of those tons and the United States 11 million tons. The Mediterranean countries such as Spain, Italy, and Egypt, as well as Mexico and China, are also leading producers.

Major U.S. Citrus Growing Areas

California and the Arizona Deserts

California grows citrus in both its northern and southern regions, as most all of the state boasts hot, dry summers and small amounts of rain only in winter. Southern California, with its many frost-free microclimates, is a traditional citrus area, and in the southern inland valleys almost any citrus can be grown. Northern California has frost-free areas as well, except along the coast where the summers are too cool and winters rainy. The inland areas of Northern California have proven fine, however, and many citrus types thrive there. The extremely hot summers, warm winters, strong sunlight, and gusty winds of the California and Arizona deserts appeal to some citrus varieties, but any fruit susceptible to burning, wind, or sun damage is at risk. In general, California orchards have long bearing seasons but require irrigation.

Texas and the Gulf Coast

These areas are usually hot and humid with some rainfall all year round. Western Texas is drier and warmer with some areas having desertlike climates. In the winter, cold waves of arctic air are common, making citrus growing tricky. Some Texas growers have been known to say, "There ain't nothing between the North Pole, Texas, and the South Pole but some barbed wire. . . ."

Florida

Florida's prolonged heat and humidity are ideal for citrus production and most regions are frost free. Rain falls in Florida throughout the year, leaving 37 to 84 inches of water on the ground each year. Before the big freezes of 1894 and 1895, the Florida citrus industry was centered in the north-central part of the state. After the freezes, the industry moved further south. Growing is now concentrated in the central section—also known as "the Ridge"—where there is an abundance of rich, high-pine soil that holds nutrients and moisture better. The coastal section (also known as the Indian River region) is famous for its sweet juicy oranges. Brevard, St. Lucie, Martin, and Palm Beach counties also produce citrus. Limes are grown exclusively in the frost-free sections of Dade County.

Climate Effects

Climate strongly influences all aspects of fruit development. Trees grow faster and bear fruit sooner in the hottest regions, whereas characteristics vary more in areas where it is cooler. Once there is fruit on the tree, heat determines how fast it will mature, which is why citrus seasons vary from region to region. More specifically, climate affects bloom, maturity, appearance, juice, and tree habits.

Bloom

Trees flower earliest in hot, humid areas and latest in cool, semi-arid coastal ones. This is seen in the way Valencia oranges reach their peak at varied points throughout the United States—in Orlando, Florida, and Weslaco, Texas, peak bloom is mid-March; in the hot deserts of Arizona and California, it is early April; in the cool coastal valleys of Southern California, early May.

Maturity

Fruit ripens more quickly in hot areas as the accumulated heat (or mean daily temperature) speeds maturity. Thus, Valencia oranges are ready to pick in February in the hot, humid climates of Florida and Texas and the hot, arid climates of California and Arizona, whereas you may have to wait until June in the cool coastal areas of California.

Appearance

Hot, humid climates produce the largest fruit, followed by hot, arid climates and then cool, arid climates. Citrus varieties that grow to a large size in the dry subtropical areas of California might be much too large when grown in Florida. Likewise, varieties such as Hamlin and Pineapple, which reach marketable size in Florida, remain small when grown in California. Fruits in warmer areas tend to be larger, whereas those in cooler areas are rounder. Peels are thin and smooth in hot, humid Florida and Texas but remain thick and tough in the arid regions of the West.

Color

Color is also affected by climate, although here heat does not necessarily produce the most vivid examples. In fact, in truly tropical areas citrus remains green when ripe. In hot, humid areas of Florida and Texas, rind color tends to remain pale. The most intense color develops in the arid climates of the West, where low temperatures prevail for several weeks before harvest and where moisture in the air is minimal. The same effect is seen in blood oranges, which color nicely in the chilly California valley evenings but fail to produce the hallmark maroon color in Florida.

The Shape of Citrus

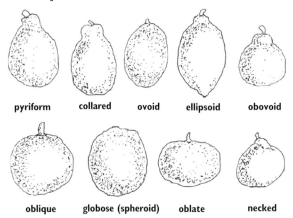

| pyriform | collared | ovoid | ellipsoid | obovoid |

| oblique | globose (spheroid) | oblate | necked |

Juice Content and Flavor

Citrus fruits are juiciest when grown in hot, humid climates and less so in regions that are hot and arid or cool and humid. The cool night air of the latter two regions keeps the fruits' acidity from decreasing. Thus, the cool nights of California result in a product that is too acidic for good juice, but one that makes a nice snack when eaten whole. High-acid varieties such as tangors grow best in Florida, where the nights remain warm.

Citrus fruits contain little starch and therefore do not sweeten after picking—hence it is important that the fruit reach its flavor peak on the tree. Sugar and acid content are the two characteristics that most determine citrus flavor, and of course, both are dependent on climate. Fruit grown in arid regions tends to have more acid and a better balance between that and sugars, which some people claim yields a richer taste. Others prefer the sweeter taste of fruit grown in humid areas, where acidity drops dramatically.

Tree Habit

The trees themselves are usually more compact in colder climates where they grow slower. This difference, combined with all the other variables, results in a southeastern variety of citrus that is lighter in color, has a thinner rind, is juicier, and tastes sweeter than the same variety grown in the West. This is why the more colorful and richer flavored California oranges are usually sold fresh, while sweeter Florida oranges are made into juice.

Citrus Fruit at a Glance

Characteristics

Knowing what to look for in specific varieties will help you when you visit your produce market, but first let's look at generic citrus as a whole. The colored skin of the rind is known as the *flavedo* or *epicarp*. Although it is edible, its pungent, bitter taste can be overwhelming. It is best used grated for flavoring. The rind is also used in pharmaceuticals and has more vitamin C than any other part of the fruit. Beneath the flavedo lies the *albedo* or *mesocarp*. The albedo contains a good deal of ascorbic acid and pectin—the latter is used to solidify jams and jellies, pharmaceuticals, and shampoos. The pulp, or *endocarp*, is the part we all like to eat, and is held together by connective tissue known as the pith. Each segment of pulp is a single carpel of the whole fruit. In the navel oranges, the tertiary fruit are additional carpels growing over the maturing fruit. The juice is contained in *vesicles* that grow from hairlike tubes on the segment membranes, filled with cells of sap.

Essential Oils

Essential oils flavor pharmaceuticals and add fragrance to soap, detergent, cosmetics, and perfumes. They are extensively used in the food industry as flavoring agents in confections, soft drinks, and liquors.

The essential oils are extracted by pressing on the outer part of the fresh peel. One well-known extract is bergamot oil, a classic ingredient in cologne and Earl Grey tea. (Steam distillation of freshly picked flowers is another extraction method, producing orange blossom water.)

Essential oils of citrus fruit have been used for centuries as folk remedies. Bergamot has been used for fevers in Italy for many years, and in China, the dried sweet orange peel is used to treat coughs and colds. In Spain, lemon oil is a cure-all, especially for infectious illnesses. In France, mandarin oil is used to treat indigestion and hiccups in children. The use of oils for aromatherapy, skin care, and as aids to circulation and digestion is also common.

Nutritional and Medicinal Value

Most of us know that citrus is an excellent source of vitamin C, and that vitamin C seems to be helpful in warding off colds. But did you also know that it is essential for healing wounds and forming collagen, which builds healthy skin, tendons, bones, and supportive tissues? Today, many doctors agree with the Nobel prize–winning work of Dr. Linus Pauling, who recommended 500–1,500 mg of vitamin C a day. Indeed, promising medical research also suggests that citrus may prove useful in the battle against cancer.

Vitamin C is water-soluble and easily destroyed. Deficiency is marked by joint pains, irritability, growth retardation, anemia, shortness of breath, and increased susceptibility to infection. Since humans are unable to manufacture their own vitamin C, it must be supplied through diet or by supplementation. This is reason enough to add citrus to your daily regime, if it is not already a tasty part of it!

Severe vitamin C deficiency results in scurvy, a disease discovered in the 1750s by a British physician named James Lind. He found that sailors on long voyages without rations that contained citrus fruits developed bleeding gums, rough skin, poor muscle tension, and slow-healing wounds, symptoms that were cured with vitamin C. On the opposite end of the spectrum, excessive vitamin C can cause kidney stones, gastrointestinal disturbances, and red-blood-cell destruction.

Citrus fruits are also a good source of potassium, which keeps muscles working properly. Oranges and tangerines are loaded with vitamin A, which plays a role in proper bone growth and night vision. Orange juice is a good source of folic acid, the B vitamin that may help reduce the risk of certain birth defects. The fiber and water citrus contains adds bulk to the diet, curbing hunger and preventing overeating.

Citrus seems very much a reflection of life. It propagates through families, but can be crossbred or hybridized with other families with remarkable results. It changes to adapt to seasons, but still maintains its consistency. It has traveled the globe full circle to propagate itself and has grown far beyond its initial varieties. It is a fruit brimming with life and parable. The hybrids and crossbreeds have brought us fruit to heal us, feed us, and sweeten our day. I hope this book impresses and amazes you with the life, vitality, and adaptability of citrus and leads you to incorporate more of its spirit into your eating, cooking, and living.

THE GENUS CITRUS

Oranges and their closely related cousins are borne by plants belonging to the genus Citrus and the genus Fortunella, of the family Rutaceae or rue. The plants are spiny evergreen shrubs or trees that bear white or purplish flowers. The fruits, classed botanically as a type of berry known as hesperidium, are clad in a leathery skin and have a fleshy interior that is divided into sections or locules. The locules are separated by parchment-like partitions. Commercially grown fruits belong to one of eight major citrus species.

Principal Parts of the Orange

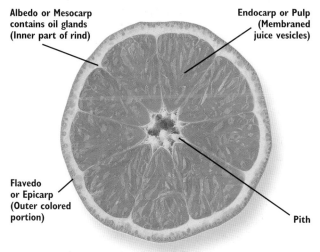

Albedo or Mesocarp contains oil glands (Inner part of rind)

Endocarp or Pulp (Membraned juice vesicles)

Flavedo or Epicarp (Outer colored portion)

Pith

C. sinensis

The sweet orange—a category which includes the popular Valencia and navel oranges in the United States, the blood oranges of the Mediterranean, and the Shamouti or Jaffa orange of Israel—is the most important member of the rue family. The sweet orange tree is a compact evergreen that grows up to forty feet and may yield fruit for sixty years or more in favorable conditions. Its pungent leaves have a glossy, wax-coated surface. Small white, fragrant blossoms appear in the spring, although some tropical climates encourage flowering all year. The small white citrus flower is Florida's state flower. The inner pulp (endocarp) consists of nine to sixteen segments filled with juice vesicles and may be seedless (Washington navel), nearly seedless (Hamlin or Valencia), or seeded (Pineapple, Parson Brown). Normally, ripe oranges contain 35 to 50 percent juice by weight, depending on variety, climate, and culture conditions. Each fruit contains 20 to 60 mg of vitamin C.

C. reticulata

More commonly known as the tangerine or mandarin, *C. reticulata* is produced from a small, thorny tree that bears simple leaves and orangelike blossoms. Its orangelike fruit, with its hybrids, ranks second to the orange in worldwide economic importance. *C. reticulata* was introduced to Europe via the Moroccan seaport of Tangier and so gained its name "tangerine" (now used interchangeably with mandarin). Tangerines are easy to peel and the segments are easy to separate. Japan grows about one quarter of the world's tangerines and exports a frost-resistant variety called the Satsuma mandarin. In the United States, most tangerines are grown in Florida. United States and South African varieties tend to have a deeper orange color to their skin and pulp.

C. paradisi

C. paradisi is the well-known grapefruit, so named because of the grapelike clusters in which this large fruit grows. The grapefruit tree is an evergreen and a descendant of the pummelo (either a pummelo mutant or a hybrid cross of the pummelo with the sweet orange). Its fruit is the largest of the commercially grown citrus and ranks fourth in world citrus economic importance.

World grapefruit production totaled over five million tons in the early 1990s, with the United States producing almost 50 percent of this amount. Israel, Cambodia, Cuba, Thailand, and Argentina follow in grapefruit production. Seventy-five percent of the U.S. crop is grown in Florida, and the other twenty-five in California, Arizona, and Texas. The white, seedless fruit and its red-pigmented mutation are the most popular varieties. Mature grapefruits reach 3 to 6 inches around and have a pale yellow rind and pale yellow or yellow-pink pulp. Juice content ranges from 35 to 50 percent of weight and is more acidic with slightly less vitamin C than orange juice. More than half the U.S. amount is canned and frozen as raw fruit or juice. Processing residues are used in peel oils, cattle feed, and various chemicals.

C. grandis

The shaddock or pummelo tree grows up to twenty to forty feet and is probably a native of Malayan and East Indian archipelagos. Named after the sea captain who introduced the tree to the West Indies, the shaddock is generally grown in tropical Southeast Asia, although two new subtropical varieties have been developed in California. The pummelo has fuzzy leaves, like those of the orange tree, and large white flowers. Its fruit is very large and, though pear-shaped, is not unlike the grapefruit with its lemon-yellow color and pungent, tart-but-pleasant flavor. Pulp segments are either pale white or red and shell out easily. Some think the grapefruit may be a descendant of the shaddock. The fruit is very popular in Asia—the Buddhists consider the pummelo sacred and the Chinese believe that placing the leaves of the pummelo in a child's bath on New Year's Eve purifies the child's soul.

C. limon

C. limon is a small tropical tree, also with white flowers that transform into a fruit commonly called the lemon. Lemons are an important source of vitamin C. Lemon trees are quite similar to orange trees but stand more upright and have scraggly branches. The lemon also profits from heavier pruning than does the orange. It has a very low tolerance for cold, which restricts the area available for cultivation. The tree flowers continuously and has fruit on the branch in various stages of development most of the year. One tree may bear as many as 3,000 lemons annually.

Most lemons ripen in the autumn and winter when market demand is at a low. Lemons are picked green, when they have reached a satisfactory size and juice content, and are then stored for sale in the spring and summer. When lemons are cured and ripened in storehouses, the fruit shrinks a little and the skin becomes thinner and tougher but develops a silky finish. At this point, they are washed, dried, and sometimes wrapped and can be kept safely like this for months.

These elliptical fruits have a neck on the stem (*peduncle*) end and a nipple on the opposite (*stylar*) end. Their rind is yellow when matured in subtropical climates. Most lemons contain 30 to 40 percent juice (mostly citric acid) depending on the variety, climate, maturity, and type of storage. The lemon is much more versatile than the other citrus varieties in adding flavor to food and drink.

Lemon cultivation has been a commercial industry in the Mediterranean for a long time. About one-fourth of the world's lemons are grown in the United States, mostly in California and Arizona. Other leading producers include Italy, Spain, Argentina, Greece, and Turkey. In the United States, the lemon grows best in the mild coastal irrigated lands of southern and central California. Many of these lemons become frozen or concentrated juice.

C. aurantifolia

Limes are small, round fruit with a thin rind, greenish-colored pulp and sharply acidic juice. A native of Southeast Asia or India, the lime is very sensitive to cold weather. Lime trees are shorter than other citrus trees and do not bear fruit until the third year. They mature fully by the age of six or seven. Most of the limes we see in super-markets come from plantations in the West Indies, Mexico, and Florida.

C. aurantifolia is the Mexican lime, also called the West Indian or key lime, a small seedy fruit. This is not to be confused with the Tahiti or Persian lime—*C. latifolia*—which is a larger seedless fruit. India has been known to produce a small ($1^1/_2$ to $2^1/_2$ inches in diameter) sweet lime with a green-yellow rind and non-acidic juice.

For centuries, sailors have eaten limes to prevent scurvy, as they are a major source of vitamin C. Lime juice is often concentrated and marketed both as a flavor-ing and as a source of citric acid.

C. medica

C. medica was the first citrus of the Mediterranean. It has white or purple flowers that produce a greenish yellow fruit six to ten inches long. The pulp is greenish and has a thick, aromatic rind, from which essential oils are derived and that is candied and used in pastries. The fruit is usu-ally much too sour to be eaten, but the juice is sometimes used to make fruit syrup. Commonly known as citron, *C. medica*, is the specific Etrog, which was struck on one side of a Jewish coin in the period of the first revolt (A.D. 66 to 77). The fingered citron (or Buddha's Hand) is revered in Asia for its fragrance and its unique hand shape. It is grown today in Italy, Corsica, Israel, the West Indies, California, and Florida, though it is believed to have originated in Mesopotamia.

C. aurantium

Seville oranges are common sour oranges originally grown in the Seville region of Spain. The sour orange was brought to Spain by the Moors in the eighth century, 700 years prior to the introduction of the sweet orange in Europe. They are grown today throughout southern Europe, the Mediterranean, and to an extent in the Americas. The sour orange was the first orange known to Western civilization. The pulp and aromatic rind of the sour orange are denser and coarser than those of the sweet orange. As you might guess, the Seville orange is not to be eaten raw! It does, however, make wonderful marmalade preserves, marinades or *mojos* (a cooked com-bination of citrus juice, garlic, and herbs), liqueurs, and perfumes.

THE GENUS FORTUNELLA (Kumquat)

Fortunella, better known as the kumquat, is native to eastern Asia and Malaysia. The kumquat is the hardiest of all the citrus fruits and is grown both for its mildly acidic (with an edible rind) fruit and as an ornamental shrub in colder areas. Its sweet-scented white flowers produce small, orange fruits, which are frequently served for dessert in China. Of the several kumquat varieties grown, the oval Nagami (*F. margarita*) is the most common. Other popular *Fortunella* include Marumi (*F. japonica*), with acidic juice and sweet rind, and the egg-shaped Meiwa (*F. crassifolia*), which is a sweeter variety cultivated in China.

Several other genera within the Rutaceae family produce fruit that is classed as citrus. For example, the small, bitter kumquat japonica is widely grown for its fruit and as an ornamental plant. The trifoliate orange, Poncirus trifoliata, is a fairly cold-hardy, deciduous citrus relative that has inedible fruit, but it is used extensively as rootstock in commercial citrus culture.

CITRUS HYBRIDS

Hybrids are the result of a cross between two fruits that differ in one or more genetic traits. For instance, kumquat hybridization includes the limequat and citangequat. Citrus trees also produce their own hybrids through spontaneous mutations. Hybrids may be intrageneric, where both parents are from the same genus, or intergeneric, where the host citrus meets another genera.

The term hybrid is also commonly used to describe a mix between fruits of different species, even though the technical name for this is crossbreeding. Most citrus is capable of crossbreeding—for example, the *Poncirus* and *Fortunella* are able to breed—although some mixes are more successful than others. Although we don't know for sure, the sweet orange is probably a cross between the pummelo and the mandarin, and the grapefruit, a cross between the sweet orange and the pummelo. Lemons most likely descend from the lime, citron, and perhaps pummelo.

Whole new citrus types are sometimes produced by crossbreeding—the tangelo (*C. reticulata x C. paradisi*) is an example. Once considered a complicated crossbreed, tangelos have become so common that they are now incorporated into the *C. reticulata* family. Citranges (*C. trifoliata x C. sinensis*) and tangors such as the king orange and temple orange (*C. sinensis x C. reticulata*) are other examples of crossbreeding. The Clementine mandarin is another fruit with a wide range of varieties, all of which are mutations of the original fruit.

The Sweet Orange

Citrus sinensis

The sweet orange is the world's most favored citrus fruit. Little is known about its state in the wild, and presumably it originated in Asia (probably what is now Myanmar and China). It was introduced to Europe as early as A.D. 200; however, the fall of the Roman Empire took European orange cultivation with it. Vasco de Gama later carried the root from India, around the Cape of Good Hope to Portugal in the fifteenth century, and so the Portuguese sweet orange was born.

By the sixteenth century, oranges had become a distinct part of the European diet. Until then, citrus was really only used for medicinal purposes, but the luscious fruit easily became all the rage. Soon the size and design of private orangeries, and the extent of their collection, became status symbols.

Spaniards introduced the sweet orange into South America and Mexico. Seeds were later distributed in Florida's St. Augustine settlement (some date this at around 1565) and by the time Florida became a U.S. territory in 1822, many orange groves were already well established. Oranges are represented by three major species: common oranges, navel oranges, and blood oranges.

Nutritional Information

Calories	80
Protein	1 gram
Carbohydrate	21 grams
Fat	0
Cholesterol	0
Fiber	5 grams
Sodium	0
Potassium	270 milligrams
Iron	1 milligram

% of USRDA

Protein	2%
Vitamin A	18%
Vitamin C	120%
Thiamin	6%
Riboflavin	2%
Niacin	4%
Calcium	4%

The flesh of the sweet orange contains a blend of sugar and acid. The sugars form during the heat of the daytime and the acids form during the cooler nights. The most flavorful fruit is found in regions with wide daily fluctuations of temperature.

BAHIANINHA

Exotic cousin to the North American Washington Navel, the Bahianinha variety is second only to the common sweet orange in commercial citrus importance. A favorite export from Brazil, this navel is smaller than the Washington and has a thinner rind casing. Its light orange rind is slightly dimpled and easy to peel. The crisp, deep orange pulp, sweet flavor, and easy segmenting make it a popular hand fruit. It is usually seedless.

The Bahianinha composes more than 30 percent of Brazil's citrus crop plantings, principally from Sao Paulo.

BERNA

The Berna is late to mature and is harvested from October through May. Although it is only moderately sweet in flavor, it is excellent for cooking due to the fact that it has virtually no seeds. Principally grown in Spain (from where it is thought to originate), this fruit is waning in popularity as it competes with the larger, sweeter Valencia. It is a medium-sized fruit with ten to twelve segments. It has a yellow orange rind, golden orange pulp, and a unique pearlike aftertaste.

When choosing sweet oranges, look for bright smooth rinds (flavedo), with a firm feel that seems somewhat heavy for its size.

CARA CARA

The Cara Cara (also known as the Red Navel) is the likely offspring of its parent Washington and Brazilian Bahia navels. The fruit and juice are a dark red color and are extremely sweet with a relatively low acid content. This Venezuelan beauty is harvested from October to January. It is a medium-sized round fruit with ten to twelve segments and few to no seeds. The yellowish orange rind and rich red pulp make it a distinguishable and appealing fruit, its appeal warranted all the more by its sweet cherry-flavored undertones. Its fleshy, crimson-colored endocarp makes it a wonderful accent to salads.

This fruit originated at the Hacienda de Cara Cara in Valencia, Venezuela.

Bahianinha

Berna

Cara Cara

DREAM NAVEL

Navels are known for their easy peeling and separation, which make them one of the finest table fruits. The Dream boasts these same attributes but is also sweeter, juicer, and less acidic than most other navels. It is harvested in October. It has a globose shape with nine to twelve segments and is often seedless. The Dream is small to medium in size, with a pale orange rind, light orange pulp, and a pleasant ripe-mango aroma.

The Dream was discovered in Orlando, Florida, which would later become home to those other dream makers at Walt Disney. The name Dream Navel was patented (U.S. Pat. No. 625) prior to release of this fruit in 1944.

GLEN NAVEL

Found on the Glen St. Mary's Groves in Polk County, Florida, the Glen Navel is one of Florida's most popular navels. The Glen is a pretty fruit—what you think of when you think of an orange. A large fruit with up to fourteen segments, it has few seeds and plentiful juice and sweetness. The Glen has a sunny orange rind and a yellow-orange colored pulp. I like the Glen for its complex palate that recalls both the mango and the papaya. It is available from October through December.

This is one of the most succulent navels—eat the Glen out of hand or juiced, and either way you will enjoy an experience loaded with flavor.

HAMLIN

This originated as a chance seedling in a grove near Glenwood, Florida, owned by A. G. Hamlin. It has become the most widely grown orange variety in Florida. This medium small globular fruit is bright orange when mature at harvest between October and January. The thin- rind Hamlin has a very fleshy pulp, making it one of the most productive oranges for processing. It is a sweet-flavored orange lacking in acid, usually with few seeds.

The Hamlin survived the great Florida freeze of 1894-1895, which brought it into greater prominence as a rival to the Parson Brown—another early maturing orange.

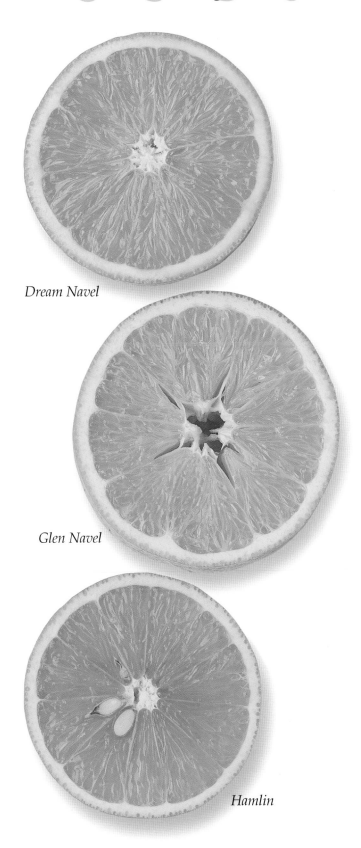

Dream Navel

Glen Navel

Hamlin

JAFFA

The exotic Jaffa was first introduced to Florida in the 1880s as a potentially cold-tolerant, high-quality, midseason species, and soon became popular. The Florida Jaffa is tender and juicy with a flavor good both for juicing and cooking. The Jaffa orange is renowned in Great Britain. Richard the Lion-Hearted, the crusader king, spent the winter of 1191–92 in the citrus groves of Jaffa. The fruit is oblique-shaped, with a slightly rough rind colored light orange covering a pale orange endocarp. The Jaffa has some seeds and is a rather small fruit with only ten segments.

*The Jaffa and another fruit of the genus **Joppa** are seedlings from the Israel Beledi tree which produced the Shamouti.*

JINCHENG

Originally introduced to the United States by the USDA for development, the exotic Jincheng is a round, smallish fruit. It generally only has ten segments, with some seeds. It has a thick, easy-to-peel rind, which when removed reveals a sweet, light orange pulp. It has a lush orange aroma with a hint of lime.

Jincheng is the most popular orange in China, where it is believed to maintain sweetness in life! Until this century, citrus fruits were expensive and so were used sparingly, yet as far back as A.D. 1200 dried citrus and orange peel were used in Chinese cuisine to add rich aroma and flavor.

KONA

The Kona orange is a Valencia introduced into Hawaii in 1792 by Captain George Vancouver. The ship's surgeon and naturalist, Archibald Menzies, raised the seedlings on board and gave them to several Hawaiian chiefs. In Kailua-Kona, some of the original stocks still bear fruit. This sweet orange is tight-skinned, round, with a solid core. The Kona has a sweet acid balance of flavor reminiscent of pineapple. The juicy pulp is divided into ten to thirteen segments. It is a late maturing fruit, harvested from March to June.

For several decades in the nineteenth century, these oranges were the leading export from the Kona district on the Big Island.

Jaffa

Jincheng

Kona

LATE NAVEL

The Late Navel is named for its January-to-March harvest—late in the season. Like other navels, the Late is known for its crisp, succulent flavor. It is a round fruit with twelve segments and about six to eight seeds. Its rind is bright orange, smooth, and easy to peel. The abundantly juicy pulp is brilliant orange and is reminiscent of a ripe honeydew melon in taste.

The navel in a navel orange is the development of a secondary fruit at the end of the main fruit, also called the tertiary fruit.

MORO

Common throughout Italy (and originally from Sicily), the exotic Moro is easily distinguished by the rich burgundy color of its juice. The Moro is quite versatile and is at home in everything from salads to chutneys to mixed cocktails. This orange has a pleasant taste and is a nice surprise on many travelers' breakfast trays. A medium-sized fruit, the Moro has a relatively long but early harvest from December through April. The rind is orange with a deep blush, and the ten to twelve segments of its fruit are nearly seedless. Moro's blood-red pulp has a sweet to tart taste with berrylike overtones.

"Blood orange" is an aggressive name for this very sweet fruit. The Moro has unequaled flavor and a remarkable coloration, which is perhaps why it is now being called the connoisseur's citrus.

MORO TAROCCO

Rich and fragrant, the exotic Tarocco is a lovely balance between sweetness and acidity and is among the best of Mediterranean fruit. The ovoid shape resembles that of the North American tangelo, or Minneola. This medium-sized, seedless fruit has a rich, juicy, raspberry flavor excellent for juicing and cooking. The original mutation occurred in the seventeenth century in Sicily, creating the striking caramel-toned endocarp. This color is due to a pigment called anthocarpium not usually found in citrus but common in other red fruits and flowers.

The Tarocco is Italy's finest orange variety.

Late Navel

Moro

Moro Tarocco

PARSON BROWN

This fruit developed in Florida from a seedling brought to Savannah, Georgia, from China. Although small, vigorous, and productive, it is usually very seedy. The Parson Brown is recognized for its distinctively thick, orange, pebbled rind, which when peeled reveals the dull yellow pulp. The saving grace of the Parson Brown is that it is abundantly juicy, with low sugar and acidity. The Parson Brown is well-suited to recipes that include citrus and has a plumlike character and taste.

This fruit was named for Reverend N. L. Brown of Webster, Florida, who discovered a chance seedling in his grove around 1856.

PERA

The Pera is light orange in color and has a firm, tough, almost rough texture that makes it difficult to eat out of hand. While the juice is vibrant and plentiful, it generally lacks richness. The Pera is a smallish oval with only ten segments and many seeds.

This fruit is the jewel of the Brazilian citrus processing industry, which yields 7.5 million tons of this variety every year.

RHODE RED

The Rhode Red is a Valencia orange; however, it exceeds the Valencia in volume of juice with less acidity (although it also has slightly less ascorbic acid or vitamin C). It was discovered in 1955 in a grove near Sebring, Florida, by Paul Rhode. Budwood put on sour orange stock caused dwarfing, and on rough lemon stock, produced large, vigorous, productive trees. In 1974, five trees were accepted into the Citrus Budwood Registration Program. This medium-to-large fruit has a deep orange color and the flavor of a juicy, ripe, delicious apple. It is round and has a dimpled rind and few seeds. The Rhode Red is available from March through June.

The Rhode Red, grown in Florida, has a more highly colored flesh than does its cousin, the Valencia.

Parson Brown

Pera

Rhode Red

ROBLE

This orange was first shipped from Madrid, Spain, in 1851 by Joseph Roble to his homestead in what is now Roble's Park in Tampa, Florida. This is a highly recommended sweet orange of superior quality, with an early harvest. The Roble is light orange in color, medium in size, often seedless, and has ten to twelve segments. The Roble has a brilliant orange pulp, which melts in the mouth with a melonlike sweetness. Look for this treat from October through the winter months.

The Roble contains 15% more sugar than any other early and mid-season variety, making it quite a sweet orange!

SANGUINELLI

Cultivated in Sicily, the Sanguinelli has a brief harvest season from February to April. It has a well-balanced flavor with a hint of sweet summer plums. Its oblong shape, golden yellow rind, and succulent red blush pulp make it an interesting-looking fruit. The Sanguinelli is common in the Mediterranean, where it's typically called a blood orange. The complex, burgundy red color of the pulp needs cool to cold weather to develop. If you manage to locate some Sanguinelli, I strongly suggest you try juicing them, as they make a deep and robust drink.

This fruit is actually a mutant of the Doble Fina and was discovered in 1929 at Almenara in the Castellón province of Spain.

SHAMOUTI

The Shamouti is a beautiful tree with dense foliage, large leaves, and no thorns—all of which endears it to home gardeners. The ambrosia of the Shamouti rivals a fine perfume, made only more spectacular by the brilliant orange hue of its pulp. The thick orange rind is somewhat dimpled and easily removed. The usual absence of seeds and the high-quality, abundant juice make it a favorite of mine for use in recipes. Shamouti is harvested in Israel from December through May. In Europe, it is known as the Jaffa orange.

The Shamouti is a mutation of an earlier and inferior Palestinian variety dating from around 1850.

Roble

Sanguinelli

Shamouti

VALENCIA

The Valencia is the most important commercial orange variety in the world—hence its "King of Juice Oranges" nickname. The Valencia probably originated in China and was taken to Europe by Portuguese or Spanish voyagers. The English nurseryman Thomas Rivers brought plants from the Azores to Florida in 1870, where the orange was quickly appreciated and cultivated first as the Brown orange and later renamed Hart's Tardiff, Hart, and Hart Late. It is rapidly becoming Florida's premier sweet orange cultivar.

The Valencia is the most satisfactory orange for the tropics, even though color development may vary in hot climates. The Valencia has a thin, somewhat pebbly, light rind. The fleshy, bright orange pulp is extremely juicy with a slight acid taste and is nearly seedless. The fruit's finish is undeniably that of the orange.

The Valencia accounts for 50 percent of the total Florida fruit crop and is the principal variety for processing.

WASHINGTON NAVEL

Originally a mutant from Bahia, Brazil, the Washington Navel orange actually traveled to North America via Presbyterian missionary, Miss F. I. C. Schneider. She was so impressed with its seedlessness and rich flavor, she sent twelve nursery-sized trees to the USDA, who in turn propagated them and offered the progeny to anyone who cared to give the species a try. In 1873 Eliza Tibbets of Riverside, California, asked that a few be sent to her for her backyard and launched the citrus industry in the western United States.

The fruit matures during the Christmas season and is generally large with a thick, easily removed orange rind. It is not very juicy but has an excellent flavor and is nearly seedless. Easy peeling and segment separation makes this the most popular orange in the world for eating out of hand or in salads. Today, it is commercially grown not only in Brazil and California, but also in Paraguay, Spain, South Africa, Australia, and Japan.

The Washington, also known as the California Navel, is the most popular navel orange today.

Valencia

Washington Navel

The Mandarin

Citrus reticulata

The word "reticulata" *actually means* netted—*a reference to the fibrous strands of pith located under the loose skin common to this type of citrus which is better known as mandarin. Mandarins are known for thin, loose peels and are so dubbed "kid-glove" oranges. They are thought to be native to Southeast Asia and the Philippines and have been cultivated in China for several thousand years. Mandarins grow most abundantly in Japan, southern China, and India. Two varieties from Canton were taken to England in 1805.*

The name "tangerine" could be applied to the whole group, but, in the citrus trade, is usually only used for the types with red-orange skin. These tangerines were well established in Italy after initial cultivation in the Mediterranean. Originally known in the west as Chinas, mandarins are among the heartiest of citrus but grow best in subtropical conditions. Many mandarins have a tendency to be alternate bearing, meaning that they yield a light crop in one harvest and a heavy one the next. There were several types of mandarin classifications used in the past for the reticulata group—the Satsuma mandarins or C. Unshiu (important to Japan), the king mandarin or C. noblis (important to Southeast Asia), the

Mediterranean mandarin or C. deliciosa, and the common mandarin or C. reticulata. Today C. reticulata encompasses the whole group which includes mandarins, tangerines, and mandarin-type fruits or mandarin hybrids such as tangors and tangelos, which are mandarin crosses with oranges or grapefruits.

Nutritional Information

✓ **5.5 ounce serving size**

Calories	45
Protein	0.92 grams
Carbohydrate	40 grams
Fat	0.32 grams
Cholesterol	0
Fiber	0.7 grams
Sodium	1 milligram
Potassium	140 milligrams
Iron	.8 milligram

% of USRDA

Protein	2%
Vitamin A	25%
Vitamin C	40%
Thiamin	8%
Riboflavin	7%
Niacin	4%
Calcium	4%

The mandarin takes it name from a group of high-ranking government officials in Imperial China, whose hats had a button shaped like the fruit and who wore orange robes.

CLEMENTINE

Mandarin

The Clementine, first grown in Algeria by Father Clement Rodier, is a cross between the Mediterranean mandarin and a sour orange. It was introduced into Florida by the USDA in 1909 and from Florida into California in 1914. It is an oblate, medium-sized fruit with few seeds. Its thick and slightly puffy flavedo is deep orange in color, with a smooth and glossy look. The Clementine separates easily into eight to twelve juicy segments filled with a taste of apricot nectar. This fine-quality fruit with its distinctive flavor has an early-but-long growing season, extending from October through March. When the Clementine is crossed with pollen of the Orlando tangelo, the tasty hybrids Robinson, Osceola, and Lee are produced.

There are dozens of Spanish Clementine varieties, of which the most popular are: Fina, the original Clementine introduced into Spain from Algeria in 1925; the Hernandina, a 1966 mutation of the Fina; and the Esbal, another Fina mutation that appeared in 1966 in Sagunto, Spain.

CLEOPATRA

Mandarin hybrid

Originally from India by way of Jamaica, the Cleopatra is also known as the Ponki or spice mandarin. It was introduced into Florida circa 1888 and is a small fruit with an odd oblate shape. Its dark orange-red peel easily pulls away to reveal six to eight segments. The endocarp is crowded with seeds—usually eight or more—and studded with green cotyledons, the first leaves produced by the embryo of a flowering plant. Cleopatra has a fine tasting apricot-colored pulp. The fruit remains on the tree until the next crop matures, making the tree almost continuously attractive. In fact, it is frequently used for ornamental landscape. The rootstock of the Cleopatra is among the most frequently used in Japan and Florida.

Cleopatra rootstock comprises about 10 percent of all new Florida citrus tree growth.

Clementine

Cleopatra

DANCY TANGERINE

Mandarin

The Dancy originated in China and is a superior fruit both for pulp and juice. Despite the fact that it has many seeds, its thin, easy-to-remove peel makes it enjoyable out-of-hand eating. This reddish-orange fruit is sweet with a tart plumlike finish. The Dancy is the leading tangerine in U.S. production, grown mainly in Florida. It is named after Colonel G. L. Dancy, who cultivated it at his grove in Orange Mills, Florida, around 1867. Although the fruit has come to take his name, Col. Dancy originally called it a "kid-glove" orange.

The Dancy was introduced to Florida from Morocco and is the tangerine traditionally associated with Christmas.

DWEET

Tangor

The Dweet is a heady, sensual fruit that grows well in California's central valley. Most consider it a cross between a Mediterranean sweet orange and a Dancy mandarin. The fruit has a medium-sized, oblate shape, with a light orange rind. It is difficult to peel but is rich in aromatic oil. Juice and seeds are abundant in the pulp. Its flavor is complex, with a plum aftertaste.

The Dweet was the result of an experiment by H. B. Frost of the University of California, Riverside.

FAIRCHILD

Mandarin hybrid

Although grouped with the mandarins, the Fairchild is actually a tangelo hybrid of Clementine and Orlando parents. Although it tends to have more seeds than most mandarins, it is always rich in juice. This medium-sized, oblate fruit has a slightly pebbly skin texture, with very firm, deep-orange colored flesh that is quite versatile for cooking. In fact, it has a distinctively tomato-like aroma! Grown in California, the Fairchild is harvested from December through March.

In 1964 the USDA introduced the Fairchild to Indio, California in the hope of cultivating a fruit with the quality of a Clementine over a long, hot summer.

Dancy Tangerine

Dweet

Fairchild

FREMONT

Mandarin hybrid

The Fremont is another mandarin hybrid introduced by the California Citrus Experimentation Station. Its deep orange rind is medium thick and easy to peel. The Fremont is a delicate fruit with up to twelve segments, and its bright reddish-orange flesh can have as many as twelve seeds. Luckily, the Fremont rewards the eater with its delightfully rich, sweet, and delectable taste, comparable to that of the Clementine.

The Fremont is most hearty and tasteful when grown in Turkey, where it sustains its abundant juiciness for more than three months after maturing on the tree.

HONEY

Mandarin hybrid

The Honey is a small mandarin with a glossy, golden-orange rind. Its flesh is flame orange, with up to twelve segments. The easily separating fruit is very juicy with many seeds.

The Honey's harvest runs from January through March.

The Honey is a hybrid of the king mandarin and the Willowleaf made by H. B. Frost of the University of California Research Center, Riverside.

LEE

Mandarin hybrid

This is a delicate fruit with an extremely limited season— only November and December. The Lee is oblate with a deep orange rind and usually has a large number of seeds in its twelve to fourteen segments. If you find it in your market, I highly suggest using it both for juice and in your recipes. The Lee's deep, fiery-orange endocarp has abundant, sweet juice and a smooth flesh texture I might call "melting."

The Lee is a cross between the Clementine mandarin and the Orlando tangelo, made by F. C. Gardner and J. Bellows in 1942.

Fremont

Honey

Lee

MINNEOLA

Tangelo

The Minneola, also known as the Honeybelle, is a large tangelo with a necked shape. The deep red-orange epicarp is thick but easy to peel. The fruit has few seeds, if any. The twelve segments separate easily and have a firm texture. The juice has a tart, honeylike sweet flavor and is prized for its quality. Tangelos are not commonly grown in California but are produced commercially and in home gardens in Florida.

The Minneola's harvest season runs from December through April. If the crop is left too long on the tree, the next crop will be light.

The Minneola is a hybrid of the Duncan grapefruit and Dancy tangerine, produced in Florida by the USDA. It was named and released in 1931.

MURCOTT

Mandarin hybrid

The Murcott is also known as Murcott Honey orange, the Red, and the Big Red. This tangor is believed to be the work of Dr. Walter Swingle and his associates at the USDA nursery. The original tree was sent in 1913 to R. D. Hoyt, in Safety Harbor (Tampa Bay), Florida, for trials. In 1922 Hoyt gave budwood to his nephew, Charles Murcott Smith, who proceeded to grow several trees. Eventually, the orange came to take his name, and by 1928 was known to several nurseries as the "Honey Murcott." Large-scale production began in 1952 to meet the high demand as fresh fruit. Because this fruit has such a thin peel, it is clipped from tree, not pulled. The glossy, smooth rind clings to the pulp but is easily removed when fresh. The tender and melting endocarp has twelve orange-colored segments. There are numerous seeds, but there is also an abundance of reddish-orange juice with a mangolike sweetness.

California produces a fruit similar to the Murcott called the "Honey," which is available at the same time of year but is slightly smaller.

Minneola

Murcott

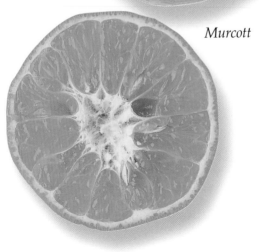

NATSUMIKAN
Mandarin hybrid

The Natsumikan, also known as the Natsudaidai, was discovered in 1740 in the Yamaguchi prefecture of Japan. The Natsumikan, probably a hybrid of the pummelo or sour orange with the mandarin, is usually much too acidic to eat. The yellowish-orange rind has a rough and uneven texture and is easy to peel. This large tough-fleshed fruit has up to twelve segments and thirty seeds. The Natsumikan is harvested from April through May.

The Japanese call this their "summer grapefruit" or "orange," and the original tree is believed to still be alive today.

NOCATEE
Tangelo

The first known tangelo was made by Dr. Walter T. Swingle of the USDA in 1897. They range in size, looking at times like the sweet orange and at others as big as a grapefruit. They are a round fruit with a tapered neck—a shape characteristic of the Minneola. This tangelo is rich and tangy with strong grapefruit notes. The Nocatee's pulp is white, has some seeds, and separates into twelve segments. It has a thick, yellow, easy-to-peel rind.

Tangelos are hybrids (both deliberate and accidental) of any mandarin orange with a grapefruit or pumello.

PAGE
Mandarin hybrid

The Page is a hybrid cross between the Clementine and the Minneola tangelo, retaining the latter's obovoid shape and rind characteristics. Its luscious red-orange pulp is broken into twelve segments and has some seeds. It is harvested from October through February—a relatively long season.

Without a doubt, the Page is one of the best for fresh juice, having tender cantaloupe sweetness.

Natsumikan

Nocatee

Page

PONKAN

Mandarin

Worldwide, the exotic Ponkan is the most ubiquitous of all the mandarins. It flourishes in locales as diverse as southern China, Formosa, Brazil, and India. The Ponkan is harvested from December through January and is large for a mandarin, with an oblate shape. Although it can have seeds (sometimes up to eight), it is aromatic, rich, sweet, tender, and melting, with an inviting salmon-orange hue.

The Ponkan is known as the Batangas in the Philippines and the Nagpur Suntra in India.

SAMPSON

Tangelo

The Sampson is an oblate tangelo cross between a Dancy mandarin and a grapefruit that is actually intended more for ornament than for eating. Its thin, yellow-orange rind is difficult to peel, and its pulp is acidic and has many seeds. The most notable thing about the Sampson is its close resemblance to the *C. paradisi*.

Dr. Walter T. Swingle created this hybrid in 1897.

SATSUMA

Mandarin

The Satsuma mandarin or *Unshiu mikan* was brought to Japan from China in the mid-sixteenth century as a chance seedling. It was later named for the former feudal province of Kagoshima of southern Kyushu, Japan. This mandarin is sweet and less acidic, with a distinct tropical fruit flavor. Being seedless with rich orange-colored flesh, it separates easily into ten to twelve segments. This early mandarin starts to mature in fall and is harvested from September through November.

The Satsuma grows well in Japan's characteristically cold citrus areas.

Ponkan

Sampson

Satsuma

SUNBURST

Mandarin hybrid

This cultivar was bred from fifteen different seedlings of Robinson and Osceola varieties. It is harvested from November through December and is a pretty, deep orange fruit abundant in juice. Getting at the pulp in this oblate, medium-sized fruit can be quite a chore due to the brittle, paper-thin rind. When seen in cross section, the beveled rind resembles the aureole of the sun (only with twelve seedy segments), hence its "Sunburst" name. Its deep color is the product of a high sugar content and high acidity.

Florida's Indian River area actually encompasses a tidal lagoon, 2 miles wide and 120 miles long, stretching from the Florida mainland and the Atlantic barrier beaches. The official Indian River area was established in 1941. It begins ten miles north of Daytona Beach and continues south through Titusville, Cocoa, Melbourne, Vero Beach, Fort Pierce, and Hobe Sound to Palm Beach.

TEMPLE

Tangor

The temple orange was originally discovered by a fruit buyer on assignment in Jamaica who was purchasing oranges after a severe Florida freeze. He sent temple bud-wood to several friends in Winter Park, Florida, who later shared it with others. Eventually, the fruit was brought to the attention of W. C. Temple (the former manager of the Florida Citrus Exchange) who cultivated and began selling it in 1919. It was not extensively planted until after 1940.

The temple's thin rind is easy to peel and has a distinctive scent to its oil. The pulp is light orange—a color that stands in stark contrast to the deeper orange color of the rind. The seeded flesh is full of robust and spicy flavor, with a tangy, tart aftertaste. Many people find the fruit appealing but too acidic. Although no one really knows for sure, the temple orange is most likely a mandarin-orange hybrid.

A tangor is a cross between a mandarin and an orange.

Sunburst

Temple

UGLI

Mandarin hybrid

Although unattractive, the Ugli is quite succulent. It has a thick, baggy, light orange rind that is easy to peel and smells of citron. The yellow-orange flesh is inviting and tender. When grown in tropical climates, the Ugli is sweet, evoking both sweet orange and tangerine. As many as sixteen large segments surround its hollow, open core—a characteristic that adds to the fruit's lack of density. Nonetheless, the Ugli can weigh up to two pounds when grown in its native Jamaica. When the Ugli (also known as Unique) is produced in a subtropical climate such as South Africa or New Zealand, the sweetness disappears.

The Jamaican exporter G. G. R. Sharp holds the copyright and trademark for the name "Ugli"—invented after a Canadian produce market called the fruit ugly.

WEKIWA

Mandarin hybrid

The exotic Wekiwa, or tangelolo, is a novelty; basically a grapefruit and Sampson tangelo hybrid, also known as pink tangelo or Lavender Gem. It can be substituted for grapefruit in any recipe, yielding a tangy-but-bright, sweet taste. The fruit has a yellow flavedo and is medium-sized with twelve segments of red blush pulp with very few seeds. The Wekiwa is harvested from November through January.

WILLOWLEAF

Mandarin

This was the first mandarin to hit the Mediterranean from China, around 1805. It was brought to England, then Malta and Sicily, before finally reaching Italy. The Willowleaf begins its harvest in October. It has an easy-to-peel light-orange rind, which opens to a flame-orange pulp that is tender and melting. The juicy, but regrettably seedy endocarp has an apricot taste and is encased in twelve sinewy segment walls.

The Willowleaf—also known as the Mediterranean—has a rind with a distinctive oil that is used by the world's perfume industry.

Ugli

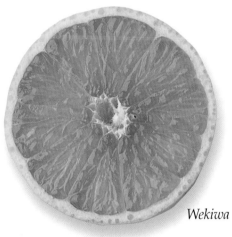

Wekiwa

Willowleaf

The Grapefruit
Citrus paradisi

Although the actual origin of grapefruit is uncertain, most citrus specialists agree that the fruit is a natural cross between a sweet orange and a pummelo. The cross probably occurred in the 1700s in Barbados. Pummelo seeds most likely arrived in Barbados by way of Philip Shaddock, an English sea captain, around 1649. There it was propagated and was known as the "forbidden fruit." Grapefruit was brought to Florida from the Bahama Islands by a French sailor named Count Odette Phillipe, who came to Safety Harbor (Tampa Bay) in 1823.

Grapefruit is grown throughout the world's tropical and subtropical regions. The United States is the undisputed leader in commercial grapefruit production and is responsible for 65 percent of the world's supply. Other important growers include Israel, Cuba, Argentina, and South Africa. There are two types of grapefruit: white fleshed and pigmented. Pigmented grapefruits do not color well in colder climates. Some varieties are seedless, though the fruit with the seeds tends to have richer, more pronounced flavor and is easier to separate.

Nutritional Information

Calories	70
Protein	2 grams
Carbohydrate	16 grams
Fat	0.1 gram
Cholesterol	0
Fiber	1 gram
Sodium	1 milligram
Potassium	210 milligrams
Iron	0.9 milligram

% of USRDA

Protein	4%
Vitamin A	10%
Vitamin C	80%
Thiamin	4%
Riboflavin	2%
Niacin	2%
Calcium	4%

Choose grapefruits that are heavy, as this indicates a high juice content.

BURGUNDY

The Burgundy has a very firm, sweet, juicy flesh that is free of bitterness, but the fruit does have a tart pomegranate aftertaste. This variety is perfect for the Indian River area climate. The Burgundy has a long harvest—November through July—but it is best if eaten from May on. The Burgundy is a patented cultivar with a Thompson parentage, although the flesh of the Burgundy is deeper and more uniformly red, and its pulp has a pinkish-bluish color. It is a round fruit of medium size with very few seeds.

Unlike pigmented, or blood, oranges, which derive their colors from cool or cold climates, the pigmented grapefruits derive their color from periods of prolonged heat.

DUNCAN

The Duncan is round and slightly oblique and can be very large. Its light yellow rind is sometimes referred to as a white in the industry. There are fourteen segments of very tender, white-to-buff colored pulp, which, although flavorful, can have as many as fifty seeds per fruit. It's not hard to understand, then, how the Duncan is used primarily for processed juice. It is harvested from December through May.

The Duncan is the oldest known grapefruit in Florida and the one from which all other varieties developed, although it was not named until 1892.

FOSTER

The Foster is great for juicing but is difficult to work with due to its numerous seeds. It is harvested from November through March and is generally medium- sized but can sometimes be very large. It is oblate and fat across the middle and has a smooth yellow rind. The Foster's pale pink pulp has a sour cherry aroma.

The Foster was the first pigmented grapefruit in Florida.

Burgundy

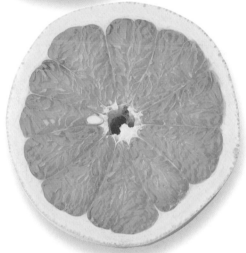

Duncan

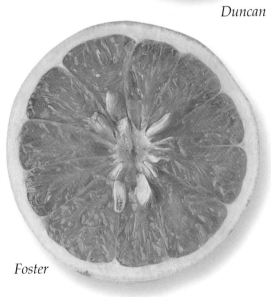

Foster

MARSH

The Marsh apparently originated as a chance seedling planted in 1860 on a farm near Lakeland, Florida. The Marsh is an average-sized round fruit with a thick yellow flavedo. The twelve segments, often with no seeds, hold a tender white flesh that is extremely rich, juicy, and aromatic. Harvested from November through May, the Marsh is the variety most planted in Florida. It is cultivated mainly for processing its abundant, flavorful juice.

The first known use of the term grapefruit occurred in 1814 in Jamaica, from which the species designation paradisi was assigned in 1830.

RIO RED

The Rio Red is a member of the Redblush variety that includes the Ruby, the Ruby Red, and the Star Ruby. All of these fruits have an intensely rich, red pulp, but the Rio Red seems destined to overtake the others in popularity and use. Originating in Texas, this is an excellent juicing fruit with a sweet and tart grape flavor. It is a medium-sized, oblique fruit with fourteen segments and very few seeds and is harvested from November to May.

This is a relatively young variety—released in 1988— that was developed in Texas to resist devastating freezes.

RUBY RED

Another Redblush, the Ruby is the most widely grown pigmented grapefruit, especially in Florida's Indian River area. Although the fruit does not process well, it is widely used for hand squeezing. The Ruby Red is medium-sized with twelve segments, few seeds, and tender, melting flesh. The taste of this juicy fruit conjures both grapefruit and orange flavors, with a pleasant litchi nut aftertaste. It is harvested from November through May.

The Ruby was the first citrus fruit ever to receive a patent—U.S. Plant Patent No. 53 by A. E. Henninger of Texas in 1934.

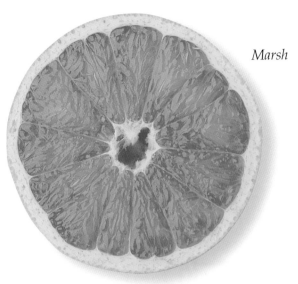

Marsh

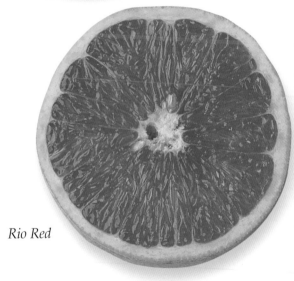

Rio Red

Ruby Red

STAR RUBY

The juice of the Star Ruby is clean and crisp and as intense as its deep, rich red color. But the positive qualities of the Star Ruby go beyond that—it is also seedless (or nearly seedless) and has a long harvest season from December through May. The yellow rind is smooth and easy to peel, revealing ten to twelve segments of pulp.

The Star Ruby was produced by irradiating seed from the Hudson grapefruit—a process used by the Citrus Center of A&I University in Texas in 1959.

TRIUMPH

The Triumph's rich flavor suggests a sweet, low acid orange. It is oblique, with a lemony yellow flavedo. The white flesh is quite seedy but rich in flavor, high in quality, and low in acid. The flavor of the Triumph suggests an orangelo—an orange/grapefruit hybrid—as it lacks typical grapefruit characteristics. The Triumph is harvested from November on.

The Triumph (circa 1884) is notable for its characteristic lack of bitterness.

Star Ruby

Triumph

The Pummelo

Citrus grandis

T he largest citrus fruit in the world, the pummelo is the botanical ancestor of the grapefruit. Also known as the C. maxima, the pummelo is native both to Southeast Asia and all of Malaysia where it grows wild on riverbanks. There is evidence that the pummelo was grown in China as early as 100 B.C.

The pummelo, which in the West Indies and the United States is known as the shaddock, remains a curiosity in Florida even though it is grown successfully in California as one of the standard seasonal specialties. It is sweeter than the grapefruit and you should use pummelos as you would a grapefruit. It is common for a pummelo to have sixteen to eighteen segments, much more than the grapefruit's twelve. The pummelo has a unique taste that is aromatic, sweet, and much less acidic than that of the grapefruit.

The pummelo can be grouped into three types by area of development: Thai, Chinese, and Indonesian. The Thai group is variable in shape and usually smaller in size than the others, though it is generally regarded as being of a higher quality. The Chinese group includes a large number of fruits, including giant oblate ones with thick rinds and plentiful juice. The Indonesian group is also extremely varied, but does tend to be larger and almost rounder than its Thai and Chinese counterparts.

The pummelo stars in one common Asian family ritual. Following dinner, the family elder carefully opens the fruit at its crown and then pulls away the outer rind. With the pitch acting as a casing, the juice sacs of the pulp are easily removed from the segments. The fruit is passed along the table so that each person can take a segment or two without allowing juice to escape or soil the hands.

Nutritional Information

✓ **5.5 ounce serving size**

Calories	60
Protein	2 grams
Carbohydrate	12 grams
Fat	0
Cholesterol	0
Fiber	.82 gram
Sodium	0
Potassium	0
Iron	0.5 milligram

% of USRDA

Protein	4%
Vitamin A	.02%
Vitamin C	100%
Thiamin	3%
Riboflavin	2%
Niacin	2%
Calcium	4%

The pummelo is the largest citrus and ranges in size from 10 inches in diameter and 4 pounds in weight, up to 25 inches and 22 pounds.

HIRADO BUNTAN

The Hirado Buntan, named and introduced into cultivation around 1960, is one of the most commercial of Japanese fruits. It is a yellow fruit that is remarkably like the grapefruit in size and shape, but its yellow-pink, blush-colored flesh is less juicy and much firmer. It has numerous segments, many seeds, and tough sinewy walls that give it an interesting consistency. The Hirado Buntan is harvested November through February.

To obtain maximum sweetness, ripen the pummelo off the tree at room temperature for ten to fifteen days, until it has a heavy aroma and deep yellow color.

LIANG PING YAU

The Liang Ping Yau is a very large Chinese pummelo. It is shaped almost like a pyramid and has a very thick, pale yellow flavedo that protects a nest of red, sweet, juicy pulp. The red fruit is encased in up to fourteen segments and has many seeds. The irregular segments create a mosaic pattern when seen in cross section. This pleasant-flavored fruit is often eaten with a honey dip in the Asian tradition. This pummelo is harvested November through March.

The pummelo is highly prized in Southeast Asia, where it is considered the best citrus for desserts and other culinary purposes.

PANDAN WANGI

The Pandan Wangi is an outstanding pummelo variety from Java's Bativia district. Its thick rind has a faint yellow-green hue and a meaty mesocarp. The blush red pulp has up to eighteen sections and eighteen seeds. The fruit yields very little juice of a complex flavor that is pleasant and sweet with a slight lime undertone. The harvest for this fruit begins in November and runs through March.

The superior pummelos grow in warm tropical regions, particularly in sheltered areas near the sea. In another testament to its heartiness, the pummelo can also tolerate brackish water and poor drainage.

Hirado Buntan

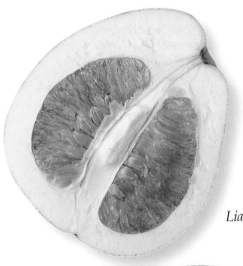

Liang Ping Yau

Pandan Wangi

PINK PUMMELO

This pigmented pummelo is a member of the Thai family. Although sometimes bitter, this fruit can have some of the best flavor of all the California pummelos. Its rind is medium thick and slightly pebbled and looks like what we call the pink grapefruit—bright yellow skin, slightly pebbled texture, many seeds, and zesty juice. Still, it is much meatier and surprisingly less acidic than a grapefruit.

The Chinese believe this delectable fruit is a sign of good fortune and prosperity, and that good things happen to those who eat it.

RED SHADDOCK

The Red Shaddock has an extraordinary flavor, very low in acidity with a sugary sweet aftertaste. Red Shaddock pulp is very similar to that of the Star Ruby—clean, crisp, and intensely red. It is a stark, grapefruit-yellow color with a smooth skin. The deep red flesh is lush and studded with many large seeds. Since the Red Shaddock lacks the astringency of a grapefruit and has drier pulp, it is ideally suited for many recipes.

This variety was only recently developed in Africa at Tambuti Estate in Swaziland.

SIAMESE SWEET

The Siamese Sweet was introduced to the United States in 1930 by the Department of Agriculture and grown at the University of California's Citrus Research Center in Riverside. The fruit is large and oblique, with a somewhat pebbly, grapefruitlike skin. Its white flesh is meaty and has few seeds. The mild juice is faintly bitter despite its deceptive name. Fruit is harvested from November through March. In Thailand, this pummelo is picked when it loses its green color and is then stored for a few months indoors to improve its flavor and juiciness.

Pummelo growers in Southeast Asia are primarily of Chinese ancestry. Traditionally, they dike the swampy land and then dredge and dig canals. These canals act both as drainage systems and transportation routes. The pummelo trees are cultivated on raised beds, in soil that has already produced quick crops such as sugarcane, bananas, and peanuts.

Pink Pummelo

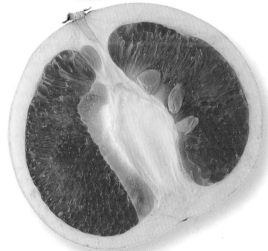

Red Shaddock

Siamese Sweet

WAINWRIGHT

The Wainwright is a California pummelo that probably descended from the Chinese group. This large, collared fruit has a lemon-lime-colored rind with a characteristic taper. The rind is moderately thick, soft, and easily peeled, revealing up to fourteen heavily seeded segments. The flesh is quite juicy with a pleasantly sweet flavor, but the pulp is somewhat coarse.

Pummelos are best eaten peeled and segmented, with membranes removed and pulp vesicles shelled out.

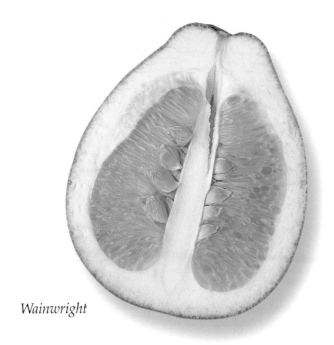

Wainwright

The Lemon

Citrus limon

T he lemon seems to have originated in either northwestern India or in the Pakistani region of Punjab. Most academics agree that the lemon was developed in the citrus gardens of Media and then carried by the Moors to the Middle East around A.D. 1150. It was grown commercially in Sicily and was brought to the Americas by Columbus during his second voyage in 1493. Some think that this Mediterranean lemon may actually be a hybrid of the citron, India lime, and pummelo.

Lemons grow best in tropical and semitropical conditions and are more sensitive to frost than other citrus. However, they also do not require much heat to mature. Unlike other fruits with defined seasons, lemons bloom and ripen fruit on the tree year-round. Most commercial lemons are grown in California coastal areas where there is an even temperature pattern. Lemons are more acidic than sweet and are commonly used in beverages, sauces, marinades, pie fillings, and preserves. Lemon and its extracts also show up in liqueurs, perfumes, and cosmetics.

Nutritional Information

Calories	44
Protein	1.5 grams
Carbohydrate	12 grams
Fat	0.3 gram
Cholesterol	0
Fiber	0.6 gram
Sodium	3 milligrams
Potassium	200 milligrams
Iron	0.9 milligram

% of USRDA

Protein	3%
Vitamin A	0.2%
Vitamin C	120%
Thiamin	2%
Riboflavin	1%
Niacin	2%
Calcium	2.5%

From Tuscany to Provence, Spain to Morocco, coast to coast in the U.S., and elsewhere around the world, the lemon is the most common cooking citrus.

BABOON

This oval fruit with a tapered neck originally was part of a USDA experiment. The Baboon originated in Brazil and has an intense yellow color to both its rind and heavily-seeded flesh. It is a highly acidic lemon with a tart taste more like that of the lime.

Lemon is a universal favorite, lending its sprightly flavor to a variety of cuisines. In the native Brazilian diet, lemon juice frequently takes the place of salt.

BEARSS

The Bearss is also known as the Sicilian lemon. It is rich and has an aromatic oil (like that of the Lisbon), which is cultivated commercially. Bearss pulp is firm and meaty with some seeds and a clean but rigorous palate. Its tart finish is reminiscent of sour berries. The Bearss accounts for 20 percent of Brazil's total lemon-lime crop and is a commercial favorite in Florida, where it is the only large variety that flourishes in the humid climate. The Florida variety was developed at the Bearss Grove near Lutz, Florida, in 1952.

*Sicily has given the world many famous culinary gems—of which sorbet is one of the most distinctive and enduring. This popular taste sensation was launched on the snow-capped peak of Mount Etna, in the tenth century, when the Moors refreshed themselves with a combination of lemon syrup and snow. The trend was particularly popular during the Sicilian summer to chill their **sarbat**, or fruit syrup diluted in ice water. The Italian **sorbetto** and the English sherbet come from these sweet syrups; this same principal is also used in most granita recipes.*

CAMERON HIGHLANDS

This fruit was discovered growing wild in the Cameron Highlands of Malaysia and was brought to the United States by the USDA. It is a small, round fruit with pale green flesh and many seeds and grows abundantly.

Commercial citrus fruit has only been harvested in Malaysia for about a decade. Until then pineapple, banana, and coconut had been given preference as they readily generated revenue. Since Malaysia's independence, citrus cultivation has been encouraged by government incentives.

Baboon

Bearss

Cameron Highlands

ESCONDIDO

This fruit was found near the Escondido River in Nicaragua and is presently being developed at the U.S. Citrus Experimentation Station. It is an elliptical fruit with a nipple at the stem and very little juice. Its rind is deep yellow and thick with a very oily feel. Although considered a small fruit, it can have up to fourteen segments of translucent flesh and as many as twelve seeds.

Need to reduce sodium intake? Substitute a squeeze of fresh lemon for the salt!

LISBON

The Lisbon is a major commercial variety that is extremely juicy and acidic. The Lisbon is so similar to the Eureka that is difficult to tell the difference between them, and so California growers cultivate both together. The Lisbon is harvested from October to August. It has a medium-sized elliptical shape with a deep yellow flavedo that is somewhat fleshy. The Lisbon's twelve segments of pale yellow flesh are wonderful to work with as they have no seeds.

True lemon characteristics—acidity, juice, color, and rind oils—do not really vary between varieties. Differences lie in their ability to survive cold and pests.

MEYER

The Meyer lemon was introduced to the United States from China in 1908. It is not actually a true lemon and a mature fruit tends to look like a large orange with a small nipple. Its flesh is a light orange-yellow color and has a sweeter juice than most lemons. It has a moderate number of seeds. The Meyer is more tolerant of the cold than other lemons and is mainly produced in the winter. Popular in California, it flourishes in the northern end of the citrus belt.

The Meyer was discovered by Frank N. Meyer, a civilian scientist who promised to ". . . skim the earth for things good for man." He was first hired by the USDA as a gardener, but after he traveled through Mexico—by foot— and studied flora there at his own expense, the USDA sent him to China as an agricultural explorer. He introduced more than 2,500 plants to the United States.

Escondido

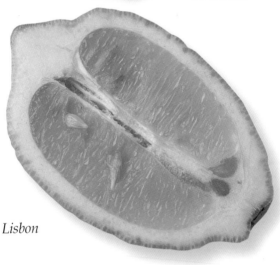

Lisbon

Meyer

VOLKAMER

In cross section, the Volkamer resembles a Sunburst tangerine, in that the rind is beveled and has a mid-orange color. Most citrus specialists agree that this is a hybrid of a lemon and a sour orange, originating in Italy. The fruit quality equals a rough lemon or Italian Monachello as it lacks juice and has a much lower level of acidity than most lemons. The Volkamer is round and small, having only eight sections and some seeds.

The seemingly natural unity of fish and lemon may have originated in Italy around 1550, when Cristoforo di Messiburgo created a recipe for marinated brill with lemon slices.

Volkamer

The Lime

Citrus aurantifolia and Citrus latifolia

L imes are produced in semitropical, subtropical, and tropical regions around the world. They originated in southern Asia and were carried by the Moors across North Africa to Spain and Portugal and later landed in the West Indies and the Caribbean. India, Mexico, Egypt, and the West Indies are major producers. Limes also flourish in coastal areas such as the Florida Keys, southern Florida, and tropical America.

Lime is a major ingredient in Caribbean and Latin American cuisine and is found in drinks, sauces, marinades, and dressings. Wedges are served with grilled fish and soft drinks. Cubans add lime to their chicken broth; in Venezuela, the favorite national dish, Sancocho, is always prefaced with lime. In Mexico, lime is added to frosty, cold beer.

Lime is used fresh in lemonade, mixed drinks, teas, and carbonated drinks. Its oil is sometimes used in cosmetics. Prior to Hurricane Andrew in 1992, 90 percent of U.S. limes were grown in Florida.

Nutritional Information

✓ **5.5 ounce serving size**

Calories	40
Protein	1 gram
Carbohydrate	14 grams
Fat	.02 gram
Cholesterol	0
Fiber	1 gram
Sodium	0
Potassium	150 milligrams
Iron	.85 milligram

% of USRDA

Protein	2%
Vitamin A	.05%
Vitamin C	100%
Thiamin	5%
Riboflavin	3%
Niacin	3%
Calcium	5%

Limes are available nearly year-round. Florida limes are most abundant between June and August; C]alifornia limes are on the market from August to February.

INDIAN SWEET
Citrus aurantifolia (Citrus limettioides)

Extensively grown in its native India, it is known as mitha nimboo. Also widely grown throughout the Mediterranean, this fruit is used principally as a rootstock. It has a yellow rind with a distinctive and aromatic oil, pale yellow flesh, and few if any seeds. Succulent, juicy, and tender, but its low acid content makes it an acquired taste. Where a Tahiti lime may have 6 percent citric acid and oranges, 1 percent, the Indian sweet lime often has less than 0.1 percent. This flat taste—although popular in the Middle East and India—is as yet lost on the United States. Harvested from fall through winter.

This fruit might be a hybrid of four separate species, including the lemon and key lime.

KEY

Citrus aurantifolia

Also known as the West Indian lime and the Mexican lime, the key lime was brought to the Americas from Asia by Portuguese and Spanish explorers in the early sixteenth century. It grows well in all of the citrus belt's hot semitropical, subtropical, and tropical regions and flourishes in the Caribbean and Florida. It is round to oval, very small, and harvested year-round. This lime was cultivated as early as 1889 in the Florida Keys. It emits an extremely distinctive aroma from its thin green rind, is quite juicy and tender with some seeds, and has a patently acid taste.

The key lime variety is referred to as the true lime.

TAHITI

Citrus latifolia

The Tahiti lime cannot tolerate frost or cold. This everbearing tree—also known as Bearss lime or Persian lime—is an ornamental variety with fragrant blossoms and dense green foliage. The fruit is oval, with a thin green rind that encases pale green, seedless flesh. The juice is plentiful but very acid, with a hint of black pepper.

Cultivated continuously in California since 1875, the Tahiti is the most valuable lime for West Coast growers.

Indian Sweet

Key

Tahiti

The Citron
Citrus medica

The citron probably originated in the same region of northeastern India as did many other lemons and limes. It was the first citrus fruit known to Europeans and has been cultivated throughout the Mediterranean from about 300 B.C. (It was originally named the "Persian apple" as all fruits were called apple at that time.) From as early as the second century, the citron has been used in cooking. The citron was among the first citrus species brought to the Americas by Columbus, although there is no commercial production of it in North America today. It thrives in Corsica, Sicily, Crete, and Israel.

The fruit of the citron is virtually inedible and neither it nor the tree is particularly ornamental. The plant itself is a scraggly, thorny shrub that is highly sensitive to cold and tends to be short-lived. The flesh, which is at times almost dry, can have either a sour or sweet palate, with a very weak lemon flavor. The peel, with its unique and resinous fragrance, has become the most used portion of the fruit and is almost always candied. It is also used in air fresheners and moth repellents for clothing.

Nutritional Information

✓ **5.5 ounce serving size**

Calories	58
Protein	0.74 gram
Carbohydrates	12.4 grams
Fat	0.5 gram
Cholesterol	0
Fiber	1.5 grams
Sodium	0
Potassium	0
Iron	0.8 milligram

% of USDA

Protein	2%
Vitamin A	1%
Vitamin C	800%
Thiamin	6%
Riboflavin	4%
Niacin	1.5%
Calcium	2%

Candied citron peel is a common food additive, used particularly in fruit cakes, sweet rolls, and candy.

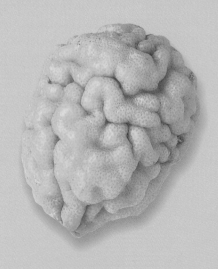

BUDDHA'S HAND

This fingered citron is called Fo Shoukan in Chinese and Bushukan in Japanese. A mutation that occurred some-time after the citron reached China in the fourth century gives the fruit its characteristic lobes that resemble the human hand. The uniquely shaped fruit is famous for its fragrance in both China and Japan and is also valued as an ornamental, ever-bearing tree.

The brilliant yellow Buddha's Hand citron is considered a symbol of happiness in China.

CITRON

Citron fruits are medium to very large and vary in shape, although they are usually oblong or blunt. The peel can be smooth but is more likely to be bumpy, yellow, very thick, fleshy, or tightly folded. It tends to be hard to peel. Unlike other citrus fruits, the citron has albedo tissue that extends between the segments and separates them. The flesh is firm and on the dry side; when there is juice, it can be acidic or sweet, as both varieties exist. The citron has numerous seeds. Oil from the peel is quite aromatic and pleasant. Salt-soaked and candied peel is used in cakes and confec-tions—most commonly in the infamous fruitcake.

The hadar, or "goodly fruit" of the Bible, is a citron.

DIAMANTE

The most distinguishing characteristic of the Diamante is its long, tapering shape, which can be up to nine inches long. The albedo is very thick and usually accounts for up to 70 percent of the fruit's shape. The flesh is coarse and usually full of seeds. When the fruit has juice, it tends to be acidic like that of a lemon.

Diamante is the principal citron variety in Calabria, Italy.

Buddha's Hand

Citron

Diamante

ETROG

The Etrog is a citron variety that is widely grown in Israel. (Both the Etrog and Diamante are acidic forms of citron.) The Etrog's yellow-orange rind is extremely thick and has an aromatic oil. The excessively seedy, sepia-colored flesh is coarse and has little juice. The etrog's flesh does have a lemony flavor. The peel of this medium-sized, oblong fruit can be candied or added to salads. Its fragrance is pervasive and can linger for weeks at a time.

The Etrog is the ceremonial fruit of the Jewish Feast of the Tabernacles, symbolizing a bountiful and fruitful harvest. Aside from commenting on its agricultural significance, the midrash says, "Just as the Etrhrog [sic] has taste and a pleasant fragrance, so there are in Israel men who are at once learned and strictly observant."

Etrog

The Sour Orange

Citrus aurantium

The sour orange originated in north-eastern India and in the adjoining areas of China and Myanmar. This was the first orange brought to Europe by the Moors, who brought irrigation technology with it. In fact, the sour orange flourished in Spain, despite the country's arid weather—and indeed, its generic name is the Seville orange. It was among the first citrus brought to the Americas. Its principal use in the United States today is as rootstock for other citrus. The sour orange has a darker and more tapered leaf than does the sweet orange and a petiole (leafstalk) that is longer and more broadly winged. Sour oranges are usually flatter than regular oranges and have thicker, rougher peels, which range in color from orange to yellow to pale green. The sour orange rind usually adheres more loosely to the pulp than does the peel of the sweet orange.

Although perhaps not the best for eating out of hand, sour oranges do have their place in the culinary world. When the peel of the sour orange is blended with fine champagne cognac, Grand Marnier is produced. Another favorite, marmalade, is made with sour oranges and has been since at least 1587, when a recipe for conserve of oranges appeared in an early English cookbook titled the Book of Cookrye.

Nutritional Information

Calories	68
Protein	2 grams
Carbohydrate	19 grams
Fat	0.3 gram
Cholesterol	0
Fiber	1.5 grams
Sodium	1 milligram
Potassium	250 milligrams
Iron	0.4 milligram

% of USRDA

Protein	4%
Vitamin A	10%
Vitamin C	120%
Thiamin	5%
Riboflavin	2%
Niacin	2%
Calcium	5%

The term "sour" refers specifically to acidity; bitter refers to the taste of the fruit's essential oils, which are also less than pleasant.

AFRICAN SOUR ORANGE

The African sour orange has a thick, pale orange rind with a green cap. It is small to medium in size and normally has ten segments. The flesh is golden orange in color and can have up to six seeds per fruit.

The amount of pectin and acid in sour oranges makes them ideal for marmalades. Homemade Seville orange marmalade is one of the most sublime confections.

ARGENTINE SOUR ORANGE

The Argentine sour orange has a thick, loose rind that surrounds sinewy segments. Seeds are plentiful and the pulp has a lemon-lime flavor. The Argentine sour orange resembles a grapefruit in cross section.

The sour orange's low sugar content, robust flavor, and potent aroma make it a popular ingredient in recipes.

BIGARADIER APEPU

The Bigaradier Apepu was originally carried to France by the Crusaders, and by 1322, Nice had begun cultivating and trading them. They were also the fruit planted in the orangeries of Versailles and Paris, making them a member of the citrus nobility. The large globose fruit has an orange, medium thick rind. Its meaty flavedo has twelve segments and many seeds with a complex juice of orange-lime flavors.

The French revolutionary Robespierre was described as sybaritic because he served "pyramids of oranges" to his guests.

African Sour Orange

Argentine Sour Orange

Bigaradier Apepu

BITTERSWEET

The Bittersweet is the Spanish principal variety of sour orange. It has clusters of acutely defined, very seedy endocarps that are encased in a thick, orange rind. The segment walls of this oblong, medium-sized fruit are tough, with an open center. The fruit is much too bitter and acidic to be eaten fresh but is used in marmalades, juice, and as an essential oil. When the leaves are crushed, they have a pleasant and distinctive aroma. In Japan, the Bittersweet is known as Daidai. This variety is also grown in Florida's Indian River area.

Orange marmalade purists insist on nothing but oranges and sugar. The pectin and acid levels of the Bittersweet variety are ideal for preserving.

CHINOTTO

The Chinotto is a beautiful fruit with a golden orange rind and deep orange flesh. It is often used as a centerpiece or an ornamental, for which it has become famous in Italy. (It is also prized for use in candymaking.) The Chinotto leaf is used in the Jewish Feast of the Tabernacles. The small fruit grow in clusters, has many large seeds, and are harvested from the fall through winter.

The Chinotto ranks with apricots and cherries as the most famous crystallized fruits from Apt, France (near Avignon).

GOU TOU

The Chinese Gou Tou has many of the grapefruit's characteristics, including its distinctive yellow skin. The fruit is oblate and has a thick rind, sinewy segments, and many large seeds. The sparse juice tastes slightly lime.

Citrus researchers suggest that the Gou Tou may become a significant disease-resistant rootstock.

Bittersweet

Chinotto

Gou Tou

SEVILLE

This is the tree that traveled to Spain with the Moors. Commercial groves exist now in most areas of the Mediterranean, with the major industry around Seville, Spain. The Seville orange is an attractive fruit with a radiant golden color in both its rind and flesh. It is medium-sized with ten large segments and many seeds. The pulp is tender but highly acidic, with a styptic effect on the tongue and mouth. The Seville's sour flavor has a distinctive bitterness, making it superior for marmalade. The juice of sour orange is often used as a marinade in Latin American countries where the trees are common. Curaçao and Cointreau liqueurs are also produced with this sour orange.

A classic Cuban mojo or marinade is made with equal parts of sour orange and olive oil, with garlic and onion added.

TUNIS

Citrus aurantium hybrid

The Tunis' full name is the "Tunisian sour orange" and the country for which is it named produces 500 acres of it yearly. The Tunis is the generic C. *aurantium* and has a thick orange-colored rind covering seedy, pale orange flesh.

Makrand is one of the most popular Tunisian sweets using this sour orange peel with dates, cinnamon, and peanuts.

Seville

Tunis

The Kumquat

Genus Fortunella

Genus Fortunella included in true citrus fruit trees was created by Dr.
Walter T. Swingle in 1915 and
named for Robert Fortune, a noted plant
explorer of the British Royal Horticultural
Society. Kumquats are called "the little gems"
of the citrus family. There are three Fortunella
types—oval, round, and large round. Another
kumquat type, the Hong Kong, is specifically
a Fortunella hindisii. Known as the "Golden
Bean," the Hong Kong is a pea-sized fruit
usually grown as an ornamental.

*Kumquat (also spelled cumquat) means "gold orange"
from the Chinese chin kan.*

Nutritional Information

✓ **5.5 ounces of edible portion serving size**

Calories	411 grams
Protein	5.7 grams
Carbohydrate	108 grams
Fat	0.6 gram
Cholesterol	0
Fiber	0
Sodium	45 milligrams
Potassium	1492 milligrams
Iron	2.55 milligrams

% of USRDA

Protein	10%
Vitamin A	75%
Vitamin C	350%
Thiamin	30%
Riboflavin	30%
Niacin	0
Calcium	25%

There is a custom in China of placing a fruit-bearing bonsai on the table, so that dinner guests may pick fruit from it between courses.

Hong Kong
Fortunella hindsii

This species grows wild in Hong Kong and in several provinces of China during the winter months. Its most distinctive characteristics are its brilliant orange color and small size—this is the smallest of the true citrus fruits. This delicate little gem measures only $5/8$ of an inch in diameter! Although the fruit is protected by many sharp thorns that can be as long as two inches, picking ripe fruit is nearly ritualistic in China.

Han Yenchin, writing in 1178, documented this "chin chu" growing wild.

Long Fruit
Fortunella margarita

This small and delicate fruit resembles the Eustis with its small oval shape and delicate, seedy flesh. The smooth rind has a sunshine yellow color and a distinctive oil. The Long Fruit has a pleasant but complex combination of acidic juice, spicy albedo, and sweet flavedo.

Kumquats are generally more tart than sweet and can add a delicate, complex taste to your recipes.

Malayan
Fortunella polyandra

F. polyandra is commonly cultivated in the Malay Peninsula, where it is known as a hedge lime because of its limelike taste. Researchers have long thought that this fruit may be a limequat, and many reference sources question its validity as a kumquat. Its rind is a deep gold-orange color that contrasts with the flame color of the flesh. This is a large fruit as compared to other kumquats and can have as many as six or eight seeds.

F. polyandra is native to the tropical region of Malaysia and is also found in southern China.

Hong Kong

Long Fruit

Malayan

MEIWA

Fortunella crassifolia (Fortunella margarita x Fortunella japonica)

The Meiwa is large, round, and plump with a lemon-hued, tart-tasting flesh. Its golden orange rind is smooth and tender and is rich and sweet as candy. The Meiwa originated in China but is grown extensively in Japan, where it is known as the *Neiha Kinkan*. Harvested from November through April, it is both pleasing to eat and prized as an ornamental plant.

Meiwa is the best kumquat for fresh, out-of-hand eating, where the rind is consumed along with the flesh. It has a lack of juice, thick albedo, and very few seeds.

NAGAMI

Fortunella margarita

The Nagami is the most popular kumquat grown in Florida. When eaten whole, it has a strong, sweet start and a slightly bitter finish. The Nagami is a vigorous and prolific fruit, with an oval shape and a smooth, bright orange flavedo. The spongy endocarp is heavy with juice and has some cotyledons. The plant's symmetrical green foliage and abundant stunning fruit make it a remarkable ornamental.

Kumquats were introduced into London from China in 1846 by Robert Fortune, a plant explorer for the British Royal Horticultural Society. The fruits were brought to Florida in 1855 from Japan.

Meiwa

Nagami

Unusual Citrus and Root Stock Fruits

Citrus has been studied and researched more than any other fruit in history. The search continues for new edible fruit varieties, improved propagation techniques, and hardy, disease-resistant rootstocks. Nearly all Citrus is cross-fertile, as evidenced by the C. reticulata and C. grandis, which are essentially born of chance. The orange Ortanique is a chance crossing between different species in the Caribbean region. Limequats resulted from a cross between Mexican limes and kumquats. One of the most well-known and tasty hybrids is the Minneola tangelo, which is a C. reticulata x C. paradisi cross. While nature has brought us some hybrids, we continue to pursue new and appealing varieties. Most citrus fruits are of the genus Citrus or Fortunella. Other true citrus fruit trees exist in closely related genera including the Poncirus and Microcitrus. There are also primitive citrus fruit trees in the genus Serverinia. Still reaching out further in the Orange subfamily, Aurantioideae, of the Rutaceae family are the Afraegle genus of hard-shelled citroid fruit trees as well as the remote citroid fruit trees of the Murraya genus.

The following fruit are among the most exotic and interesting in the world.

Intergeneric breeding is the most important step in developing new, stronger, and more disease-resistant rootstocks.

AUSTRALIAN FINGER LIME
Microcitrus austalasica

The Australian finger lime could be classed as either a tall shrub or small tree. Its spiny foliage makes it a fine Australian ornamental. This tiny citrus variety has many lime characteristics, and its fruit is long and cylindrical in shape. Oil seeps from the rind into the pulp, giving the fruit its very acidic flavor and lingering aftertaste.

*This fruit is somewhat like **Beauty and the Beast**, with its pleasant lemonlike flavor and its turpentine-esque aftertaste.*

BOX ORANGE
Citrus buxifolia **and** *Severina*

The box orange also goes by the more romantic name of Severina. The fruit is nearly black and grows in clusters like berries. It is from a family of six species that include *buxifolia, buxifolia brachhytic, disticha, linearis, paniculata,* and *retusa*. The tree is distributed mainly in the Philippines, Malay Peninsula, India, and New Guinea, where it is used only as an ornament as its fruit is inedible.

In China, the box orange leaves are used to make yeast cakes called tsau ping lak, meaning wine cake thorn in Cantonese.

CALAMONDIN
Citrus madurensis loureiro

The Calamondin originated in China and was introduced into Florida as an "acid orange" around 1900. It closely resembles the mandarin with its small, oblate shape and flattened or depressed ends. The peel is thin, smooth, and bright orange and separates easily from the fruit. Its juicy and acidic flesh matches the rind in color. There are five to nine segments with seeds and cotyledons grouped around a small, semihollow axis. The Calamondin grows wild in Asia and the Philippines, where it is called "cala-monding." In Hawaii, it is known as "kalamansi."

"Dooryard fruit" are so named because they are easy and common enough to grow in your own home garden.

Australian Finger Lime

Box Orange

Calamondin

CITRANGEQUAT
Fortunella sp. x (Citrus sinensis x Poncirus trifoliata)

The Citrangequat is a trigenic hybrid cross between the trifoliate orange, sweet orange, and kumquat. It is grown as the Thomasville in Florida. The blaze-orange rind of this pear-shaped fruit is quite pebbly, covering golden flesh. The small fruit is somewhat acidic and seeded, unless fully mature, when it is sweet enough for eating fresh out of hand.

The Citrangequat was developed at the turn of the century in the hopes of producing a fruit with the hardiness of the trifoliate and the sweetness of the sinensis.

EUSTIS
Limequat (Fortunella x C. floridana)

The Eustis is an elliptical fruit with Mexican lime and Marumi kumquat or limequat parentage. The flavedo is smooth and lemon-yellow in color. The sunbright yellow flesh has up to eight segments with as many as eight small seeds. The juice is sweet and plentiful given the fruit's small size—the Eustis looks a lot like a jumbo olive. The plant is used mostly as an ornamental and grows in Florida from November through July.

This is an excellent decorative plant with the scent of lime.

FLYING DRAGON
Poncirus trifoliata (Trifoliate)

The Flying Dragon is the most important and interesting of all the dwarfed ornamental varieties. Also called the Japanese hiryo, this plant was introduced to the United States in 1915. Although it bears lovely large and fragrant blossoms in the spring, it is mostly considered a curious monstrosity with its severe-looking limbs and jagged thorns. The botanical variety is *monstrosa* of Tokutaro Ito. The Flying Dragon bears a golfball-sized inedible fruit with a rough orange rind. Its flesh is pale yellow and has six to eight sections and many seeds.

Trifoliate orange is a spiny deciduous shrub, which is a common rootstock that is extremely hardy in winter.

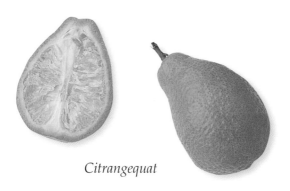

Citrangequat

Eustis

Flying Dragon

I CHANG

Citrus ichangensis

Known formally as the "Ichang papeda," this truly extraordinary plant grows wild in southwestern China. It is oblong in shape and has a rough, pale orange rind. The thick mesocarp holds meaty flesh that is packed with many seeds. The I chang is used like a lemon.

The I chang is reported to have survived subzero temperatures.

KAFFIR LIME

Citrus hystrix

The Kaffir lime is a popular ingredient in Asian cooking, particularly in Laos, Cambodia, and Thailand. As Asian immigrants continue to come to the United States, a new demand for the Kaffir lime has prompted growers in California to begin cultivating it. Also known as Kieffer and Kuffre, the Kaffir fruit is small and round, with a thick, bumpy, and tough rind. The pale green flesh is full of seeds and sour juice.

The long, slender, notched leaves of the Kaffir are used like bay leaves in Pacific Rim cuisine.

LEMONQUAT

Fortunella sp. x C. limon

A hybrid of the lemon and the kumquat, the lemonquat has a pearlike shape and smooth rind. A cross section reveals the daisylike pattern of its thick mesocarp. The fruit has eight segments of orange-yellow flesh, with many seeds and some juice.

I Chang

Kaffir Lime

Lemonquat

NASNARAN

Citrus amblycarpa

Outwardly, this fruit has the characteristics of a sour orange—its rind is light orange and pebbly, with a dimple at the stem. It is a medium-sized fruit with up to twelve segments. The pale yellow flesh usually has one large seed per segment.

NEW GUINEA LIME

Microcitrus waburgiana

This exotic-looking, leafy plant has elongated crescent-shaped fruit. The deep green rind covers a pale green flesh with several seeds. This microcitrus has no segments but is instead one large collection of carpels.

This is the only species of the genus Microcitrus outside of Australia.

NIGERIAN POWDER FLASKS

Afraegle paniculata

The Nigerian Powder Flask is part of a West African group of hard-shelled, citrus-like ball fruit. The trees can grow as high as 16 feet, and are found in villages through-out Benin and Nigeria. The seeds are edible and contain an essential oil. The fruit is small—with only eight segments—and full of these seeds.

NIPPON ORANGEQUAT

C. reticulata satsuma x Fortunella margarita medua

The Nippon is a medium-sized, mildly flavored fruit. This orangequat has a thick, red-orange rind that is sweet and edible, and its sweet, meaty pulp has a slight acidic after-taste. Its six sections are well defined and have some seeds. Harvested from December through September, the Nippon orangequat can be used in marmalades or candied.

The name given to this hybrid is misleading since its parentage is of mandarin rather than orange.

Nasnaran

New Guinea Lime

Nigerian Powder Flasks

Nippon Orangequat

ORANGE JASMINE

Murraya paniculata

This exotic shrub is found throughout India, Sri Lanka, Myanmar, China, and Australia. The species grows as an evergreen and is used most often as a greenhouse ornament.

Although there are many varieties and strains of Murraya, the orange jasmine is the most common. The cranberry-red fruit has an ovoid shape, one to two seeds, and is only a half-inch in diameter. It buds a striking white flower that is fragrant and rich in essential oil.

*The **Murraya** genera are remote citroid fruit trees in the orange subfamily.*

ORTANIQUE

Citrus x nobilis

The Ortanique was discovered in Jamaica, as were its cousin tangors, the temple orange and the Ugli. Climate affects the look, feel, and taste of this fruit dramatically. In tropical Jamaica, the fruit is seedless and pale orange in color, with juicy, sweet orange overtones and a thin rind. In Mediterranean Israel, it has some seeds, a fairly thick rind, and a mid-orange color. In semitropical Cyprus, it has a deep orange color, many seeds, and thicker rind.

The name is an amalgam of OR(ange)TAN(gerine)(un)IQUE.

PROCIMEQUAT

C. aurantifolia x Fortunella japonica x Fortunella hindsii

The procimequat is a cross between the Eustis limequat and the *F. hindsii*. This small, round fruit grows in clusters on thorny branches with long, deep green leafs. The smooth orange rind is soft and easy to tear. The flesh is dense and contains a few seeds and cotyledons.

This is one of the fruits leading the study of true bigeneric backcrosses and a trigeneric hybrid— PRO(to)C(itrus) (L)imequat.

Orange Jasmine

Ortanique

Procimequat

RANGPUR

Citrus limonia Osbeck

The Rangpur was imported from India (where it originated) to Florida in 1887. Its greatest selling points are its rootstock and use as an ornamental. Rangpur lime is a highly acidic fruit that resembles the mandarin in appearance, and in fact, it is also known as mandarin lime. It is a tender and juicy oblate fruit with a rather complex tangerine-lime flavor. The Rangpur's rind is reddish-orange, surrounding a deep orange flesh with seeds.

In India, mandarin juice is improved by adding 20 to 40 percent Rangpur juice to it.

SINTON

Citrangequat

This oval kumquat and Rusk citrange hybrid was first bred in Sinton, Texas, from where it gets its name. It is an attractive ornamental plant with brightly colored but highly acidic fruit. The fruit has a tapered neck and a striking orange rind, and the flesh is lemon yellow with a few seeds. The Sinton is harvested from December through March.

Roll the fruit in your fingertips to combine the sweet flavors of the skin with the tart flavor of the pulp.

SYDNEY HYBRID

M. australias x australasica

The Sydney is a hybrid cross between the Australian round lime and one finger lime. The green, elongated fruit is acidic and seedless. New growth is purple with red buds and a spicy odor. Combine these colors with the Sydney's slender, thorny twigs and you have the makings for a popular and colorful ornamental.

The pulp of the Sydney is reminiscent of glistening green caviar eggs.

Rangpur

Sinton

Sydney Hybrid

Recipes

Introduction

To create my New World cuisine, I work with a far-reaching collection of ingredients to achieve a balanced composition of textures, colors, and flavors. Citrus is one of the wonderful ingredients I use frequently to provide this balance. I especially love the pastel colors of citrus in contrast with other foods.

Traditionally, citrus is most often used in its raw form and as a beverage. Oranges are simply cut in quarters or peeled and segmented, and grapefruits are mostly cut in half. Tangerines and mandarins are served in segments and lemons and limes as wedges. Freshly squeezed and concentrated citrus juices are used as beverages and bar mixers. We often relegate citrus juices to breakfast, despite the contributions they can make to other meals.

Too often our cooking is limited to a few familiar fruits, spices, and herbs. I find myself breaking free of these traditional restraints in my search for new citrus uses. After reading these recipes, you will find citrus pulp, juices, zests, and oils easy to add to your repertoire. You will be able to use citrus in new ways to create marinades, salsas, mojos, relishes, chutneys, and sofritos (a combination of vegetables and spices used as a base for further cooking).

Keep in mind that citrus is interchangeable in recipes. You may substitute one type of orange for another or one lime for another lime. You can use grapefruit instead of pommelo or orange instead of tangor. A combination of orange and lime juice may be used to replace sour orange. You may even use lemon in a recipe that calls for lime—just use your imagination, and don't worry if you can't find the exact varieties specified here. Obviously, there will be certain changes in taste when you make substitutions but in most cases substitutions work very well.

The taste buds located on different areas of your tongue can distinguish between four separate aspects of flavor—sweet, salt, sour, and bitter. Citrus has the unique quality of reacting simultaneously on many of these areas. We humans seem to have an innate liking for sweetness and a dislike for bitterness. All you need to know to use citrus effectively is that citrus flavors are a balance of sugar and acid (sweet and sour).

The acid balance or sourness in a dish is very important. You will find you can perk up or add pizzazz to the flavor of a dish with an added squeeze of lemon or lime. The addition of an acidy citrus brings out the best in a spicy hot dish, like Star Anise Chicken Wings with spicy Tangerine Salsa. The citrus can also bring out the full flavors of a dish like Skirt Steak with Zinfandel Mojo and Salsa Turned Orange. Many of us love a squeeze of lemon on a simply grilled lobster.

In the Caribbean islands, people add lime to finish a roasted chicken, and here I use it for Spicy Green Coconut Rice. A vinaigrette is a clear example of an acid-balanced sauce and actually requires less oil when fresh citrus is used. A simple lemon vinaigrette made with two parts olive oil to one part freshly squeezed lemon juice adds a new dimension to fresh greens. The Citrus Sofrito Cruda is one of my favorite unique vinaigrettes.

Cooking with citrus can be as simple as cooking with other acidic foods, such as wine, vinegar, or tomatoes. Just as too much wine will make a dish sour, so will citrus. When cooking a savory dish with citrus you have to consider both the acid and sugar levels. Use the flavor components to enhance the other elements of the dish, as in Pommelo Pork Chops. Citrus can be used raw either to marinate or to enhance the finish of the dish, as in Tuna Poke with Key Lime and Coconut. Or citrus can be used to cut through the richness of beef as I do with Citrus Barbecue Short Ribs. The sweet and sour flavors of ancient Asia have traveled with the citrus for many years and through many cultures.

Small Bowls and Tall Glasses

Starters

Mains

Desserts

Salsas, Mojos, Marmalades Relishes, and Chutneys

Cuban Rum Cocktail

Mojito

This refreshing cocktail has its origins in Havana. It is based on three cornerstones of commerce in old Cuba: citrus, sugar, and rum. Lime also plays a key role in Cuban cuisine.

➤ *Serves 1*

1 tablespoon freshly squeezed lime juice
1 (2-inch) piece lime zest
1 teaspoon sugar
1 sprig fresh mint, plus 1 leaf for garnish
1½ ounces white rum
Ice cubes
½ cup club soda

In a medium-sized glass combine the lime juice, zest, sugar, mint, and rum. Stir and add the ice and club soda to fill the glass. Serve garnished with the mint leaf.

Orange-Mango Smoothie

Batido

A batido is a Latin interpretation of a fresh fruit smoothie. Orange juice brings the flavor to a satisfying balance of sweetness and acidity.

➤ *Serves 2*

½ cup whole milk
1 cup cubed fresh mango
1 banana
½ cup freshly squeezed orange juice
1 cup crushed ice
1 teaspoon honey
2 slices sweet orange, for garnish

In a blender, combine all the ingredients except the orange slices and blend until smooth. Pour into 2 tall glasses and garnish each with an orange slice.

Green Apple Lemonade

I love the crisp tartness of chilled Granny Smith apples. This lemonade is healthy and wonderfully refreshing—it will keep you going for the rest of the day.

➤ *Serves 2*

3 large Granny Smith apples, peeled and cored
Juice of 2 large lemons
1 tablespoon sugar
1 cup cold water
Ice cubes

Using a juicer, extract the juice from the Granny Smith apples. In a small pitcher, combine the fresh apple juice, lemon juice, sugar, water, and ice. Mix well and pour into 2 tall glasses.

Orange and Carrot Juice

Jugo de Naranja

One glass of freshly squeezed orange juice in the morning is part of a satisfying breakfast. Try this simple combination of orange and carrot juices as a change of pace.

➤ *Serves 2*

3 large carrots, trimmed and peeled
4 large oranges, halved
Pinch of sea salt
2 lime wedges

Using a juicer, extract the juice from the carrots. Chill the carrot juice in the refrigerator. Using a juicer or wooden reamer, squeeze the oranges into a small pitcher. Add the carrot juice, season with salt, and mix well. Pour into 2 tall glasses and garnish each with a wedge of lime.

Ugli Fruit Soup

The hearty citrus flavor of Ugli fruit inspired this soup—it was one of the first exotic citrus flavors I experienced in southern Florida. I discovered that the flavor peaks in this warm broth.

➤ *Serves 4*

1 large Ugli fruit
1 large orange
$\frac{1}{2}$ cup honey
$\frac{1}{2}$ teaspoon grated gingerroot
$\frac{1}{2}$ cup water
2 cups freshly squeezed orange juice
2 cups weakly brewed orange pekoe tea
2 teaspoons arrowroot
$\frac{1}{4}$ cup freshly squeezed lemon juice
2 tablespoons freshly squeezed lime juice
$\frac{1}{2}$ teaspoon kosher salt

Cut four strips, each 3 inches long and 1 inch wide, from the peels of the ugli fruit and the orange. Julienne the strips. Peel the remainder of the fruits and separate them into sections. Set aside both peels and sections.

In a medium-sized saucepan, combine the honey, ginger, ugli fruit and orange peels, and water. Stir over low heat until the honey is dissolved, raise the heat and bring to a slow simmer. Cook for approximately 15 minutes, until the peels are translucent. Stir in the orange juice and tea.

In a small stainless steel bowl, combine the arrowroot, lemon juice, and lime juice, and stir until the arrowroot is dissolved. Add this to the soup mixture and mix well. Bring to a boil, then lower the heat and simmer for 5 minutes. Season with the salt.

To serve, place the segments of Ugli fruit and orange in 4 bowls. Pour the soup over and serve hot.

Calabaza Mojo Soup
with Toasted Brazil Nut Chips

In this soup, I combine flavors of the orange mojo and Scotch bonnet chile with rich calabaza, West Indian pumpkin. The winter-time flavors of calabaza and oranges are meant for each other.

➤ *Serves 6*

1/4 cup olive oil

1 onion, diced

1 tomato, peeled, seeded, and chopped

1/2 teaspoon chopped garlic

1 small Scotch bonnet chile, seeded and chopped

2 pounds calabaza, peeled and cut into 1/2-inch cubes

2 cups orange juice

3 cups vegetable stock

2 teaspoons kosher salt

1/2 cup shelled Brazil nuts

In a large pot over medium heat, warm 3 tablespoons of the olive oil. Add the onion and cook until translucent, about 5 minutes. Add the tomato, garlic, and chile, and cook for 5 minutes. Add the calabaza, orange juice, and stock, and bring to a boil. Lower heat and simmer for approximately 25 to 30 minutes, stirring frequently, until the calabaza is very soft, thickening the soup. Season with 1 1/2 teaspoons of the salt.

Meanwhile, to prepare the chips, preheat the oven to 350°. In a small pot, cover the nuts with water and bring to a boil. Reduce heat and simmer for 3 minutes. Remove from heat and drain. With a sharp paring knife, cut or shave the nuts lengthwise into very thin chips. On a baking sheet, lay the chips in a single layer, drizzle them with the remaining tablespoon of olive oil, and sprinkle with the remaining 1/2 teaspoon of salt. Bake for approximately 4 minutes, until chips are golden brown. Remove from oven. Serve immediately as a garnish to the soup.

Tuna Poke *with Key Lime and Coconut*

Poke is a preparation of extremely fresh fish or seafood, simply marinated and chilled. This particular recipe sparkles with the tropical highlights of key lime and coconut.

➤ *Serves 4*

2 tablespoons minced gingerroot

1 teaspoon minced garlic

2 tablespoons sesame oil

1 tablespoon minced hot Thai chile or jalapeño

2 tablespoons minced green onion

2 tablespoons minced fresh cilantro

2 tablespoons soy sauce

1 pound fresh tuna filet, diced into medium-sized chunks

2 tablespoons key lime juice

$1/4$ cup toasted shaved coconut

In a large bowl, combine the ginger and garlic. Heat the sesame oil in a small pan. When it is hot, pour it into the ginger and garlic and mix well. Add the chile, green onion, cilantro, soy sauce, and tuna, mixing well. Cover and chill for 2 hours.

Just before serving, stir in the key lime juice and toasted coconut.

Tangor Shrimp Ceviche

Ceviches, which are based on citrus, came into use centuries ago as a method for preserving fish and shellfish. In this recipe, marinating the shrimp in citrus juices effectively "cooks" them. The use of several types of citrus—including the exotic tangor—enhances the flavor of this ceviche.

➤ *Serves 4*

1 pound peeled, cleaned, and butterflied medium shrimp
1 cup freshly squeezed lime juice
$^1/_2$ cup freshly squeezed orange juice
1 medium sweet onion, thinly sliced
4 large plum tomatoes, peeled, seeded, and diced
1 medium jalapeño, seeded and diced
2 large tangors, peeled, seeded, and divided into segments
2 tablespoons chopped fresh cilantro
2 teaspoons kosher salt
2 heads Belgian endive

In a small stainless steel bowl, combine the shrimp with the lime and orange juices and mix well. Cover and refrigerate for two hours.

In another stainless steel bowl, combine the onion, plum tomatoes, jalapeño, tangors, and cilantro. Season with kosher salt and cover. Add the shrimp and half of the juice marinade to the fruit mixture.

To serve, separate the spears of Belgium endive into 4 tall cocktail glasses and spoon the ceviche into the glasses.

Warm Portobello Escabeche *with Yuca Mojo, Green Olives, and Shaddock Salad*

Although the traditional escabeche is a pickled fish, I use meaty portobello mushrooms to bring a new dimension to this classic dish. You may substitute half sweet orange and half lime juice if you can't find Seville sour oranges.

► *Serves 4*

4 large portobello mushrooms

3 tablespoons olive oil

1 teaspoon chopped garlic

$1/4$ teaspoon black peppercorns

$1/4$ teaspoon kosher salt

2 tablespoons red wine vinegar

$1/4$ teaspoon ground allspice

$1/4$ teaspoon chopped fresh thyme leaves

$1/2$ cup Seville orange juice

$1/2$ cup dry white wine

Yuca Mojo, Green Olives, and Shaddock Salad (see page 152)

Remove and discard the stems from the mushrooms just under the caps. In a large sauté pan, warm the olive oil. Place two mushroom caps at a time in the pan and cook for approximately 2 minutes on each side. Return all four mushrooms to the hot pan. Add the garlic and the remaining ingredients except the Yuca Mojo, Green Olive, and Shaddock Salad. Simmer for 3 to 4 minutes until the mushrooms are softened. Remove the mushrooms to a platter. Continue to simmer the cooking liquid until it is reduced by half. Pour the reduction over the mushrooms and let cool.

The mushrooms can be served at room temperature or refrigerated overnight to be served the next day. Serve with the Yuca Mojo, Green Olives, and Shaddock Salad.

Ginger Grilled Grapefruit
with Orange Blossom Honey

From the French, I learned the beauty of contrasting temperatures and textures, as exemplified by the classic grilled grapefruit dish, Pamplemousse au Cassis. *In this version, the sparkling grapefruit flavor is enhanced by the combination of sesame, ginger, and honey.*

➤ *Serves 4*

2 large Ruby Red grapefruits
2 teaspoons light sesame oil
1 teaspoon minced gingerroot
$\frac{1}{4}$ teaspoon kosher salt
$\frac{1}{8}$ teaspoon freshly ground black pepper
1 tablespoon light brown sugar
4 tablespoons orange blossom honey
$\frac{1}{2}$ teaspoon sesame seeds, toasted

Remove the skin and pith from the grapefruits and cut the flesh into 1-inch-thick wheels. Remove the seeds and arrange the slices on a broiler tray. In a small bowl, combine the sesame oil, ginger, salt, pepper, and brown sugar. Brush the grapefruit with the seasoned oil.

Preheat the broiler or grill until very hot. Grill the grapefruit slices on one side for approximately 2 minutes, until the sugar begins to caramelize. Remove from the heat.

To serve, arrange the fruit on a warm platter. Drizzle with the honey and sprinkle with the toasted sesame seeds.

Stamp and Go *with*
Calamondin–Green Mango Chutney

*Stamp and Go is a whimsical Jamaican name
for the salt cod fritters eaten throughout the
Caribbean. The best way to handle salt cod is to
soak it in cold water. After 12 hours, rinse and
cover with fresh cold water. After soaking the
fish for a total of 24 hours, remove the salt cod
from the water. By hand, shred the flesh into a
bowl, removing any skin or bone.*

➤ *Serves 10*

2³/₄ cups all-purpose flour
1 teaspoon baking powder
1 tablespoon orange blossom water
1³/₄ cups water
³/₄ cup chopped onion
¹/₂ teaspoon chopped garlic
3 tablespoons chopped fresh cilantro
3 tablespoons minced fresh chives
¹/₂ teaspoon chopped Scotch bonnet chile
1 tablespoon chopped gingerroot
3 tablespoons freshly squeezed lime juice
1 pound salt cod, soaked and shredded (see above)
1 cup peanut oil
1 cup Calamondin–Green Mango Chutney (see page 147)

Combine the flour and baking powder in a stainless steel
bowl. Add the orange blossom water and water and mix
together with a wooden spoon until just combined. Add
the onion, garlic, cilantro, chives, Scotch bonnet, ginger,
and lime juice. Mix in the salt cod until smooth. Cover
and refrigerate for at least 30 minutes.

Warm the peanut oil in a heavy cast iron pan on medium heat. When the oil is hot, spoon in the fritter mixture
with a tablespoon, cooking about 6 to 8 fritters at one
time. Cook approximately 3 minutes, or until well
browned. Turn the fritters with a spatula and brown the
second side well for another 2 minutes. Remove the fritters from the pan and pat them dry with paper towels.
Serve hot with Calamondin-Green Mango Chutney.

Star Anise Chicken Wings
with Spicy Tangerine Salsa

An old Chinese cook in Chinatown introduced me to the wonders of star anise, which is wonderful paired with chicken. This earthy, exotic licorice spice is also a great companion to citrus flavors like tangerine.

➤ *Serves 4*

2 tablespoons star anise seed

$1/2$ teaspoon cumin seed

$1/2$ teaspoon black peppercorns

1 teaspoon chopped garlic

1 cup Chinotto sour orange juice

1 pound chicken wings

2 quarts peanut oil (for deep-frying)

1 teaspoon chopped lemon zest

3 tablespoons soy sauce

1 tablespoon dark sesame oil

3 tablespoons dark brown sugar

$1/4$ teaspoon cayenne

1 cup Spicy Tangerine Salsa (see page 149)

Using a spice grinder or clean coffee grinder, grind the star anise, cumin, and peppercorns. In a stainless steel bowl, combine half the star anise mixture with the garlic and orange juice. Reserve the remaining star anise mixture. Add the chicken wings, cover, and refrigerate for at least 1 hour.

Fill a deep fryer with the peanut oil. Preheat the oil to 375°. Drain the wings and fry them in small batches until crisp and golden brown, approximately 3 to 4 minutes. Drain on paper towels or a slotted pan.

In a stainless steel bowl, combine the remaining star anise mixture, lemon zest, soy sauce, sesame oil, brown sugar, and cayenne. Toss the cooked chicken wings into the seasoning and mix well.

To serve, arrange the crispy wings on a platter and serve with Spicy Tangerine Salsa.

Lemon Red Snapper
with Spicy Green Coconut Rice

The combination of citrus in the marinade and time spent marinating at room temperature means that the snapper actually starts cooking as it sits on the countertop.

➤ *Serves 4*

- 2 (2 pound) whole red snappers, scaled and cleaned
- 2 large lemons, zested and juiced
- 4 ounces dry sherry
- 1/2 cup finely diced Spanish onion
- 4 tablespoons olive oil
- 1/2 teaspoon kosher salt
- 1/2 teaspoon coarsely ground black pepper
- 1/4 cup pine nuts
- 2 teaspoons chopped chives

Spicy Green Coconut Rice

- 1 tablespoon olive oil
- 1 cup chopped Spanish onion
- 1/2 cup seeded and diced green New Mexico or Anaheim chiles
- 1 teaspoon chopped garlic
- 1 1/2 cups uncooked long grain rice
- 1/4 cup coconut milk
- 3 cups water
- 2 teaspoons kosher salt
- 1/2 teaspoon ground black pepper
- 1 teaspoon ground cumin
- 2 tablespoons shaved, unsweetened coconut flakes
- 2 tablespoons chopped fresh cilantro leaves
- 1 cup chopped leaf spinach
- 1 large lime, zested and juiced

Wash the fish in cold water and drain. Score the flesh 3 times on each side, approximately 1/2 inch deep and 3 inches long. In a stainless steel bowl, combine the lemon juice, sherry, onion, 3 tablespoons of the olive oil, salt, and pepper. Pour this mixture over the snapper and rub into the flesh. Marinate for 30 minutes at room temperature.

To cook the rice, heat the oil in a heavy saucepan. Add the onion and cook over low heat until the onion turns translucent, approximately 5 minutes. Add the chiles, garlic, and rice, and mix until evenly coated. Add the coconut milk, water, salt, pepper, and cumin. Stir well and bring to a simmer. Cover the pot and simmer slowly for 20 minutes. Remove the pot from the heat. Fluff the rice with a fork and add the coconut, cilantro, spinach, lime, and lime zest.

Preheat the oven to 400°. Place the fish in an ovenproof pan with marinade and bake, moistening the fish with marinade every 3 minutes. Bake for approximately 10 to 12 minutes, until flesh begins to flake to the bone. Remove the snapper to an oversized colorful dish and reserve the marinade.

Combine the lemon zest and pine nuts with the remaining olive oil in a small ovenproof pan. Bake for 2 to 3 minutes until lightly browned and aromatic. Sprinkle over the fish, along with the chives and reserved marinade. Serve with the rice.

Blasted Shrimp
with Meyer Lemon Date Relish

In this deceptively simple recipe, the shrimp are literally "blasted" with a rapid searing heat to seal in their sea-kissed flavor and juices.

➤ *Serves 4*

> 1 tablespoon olive oil
> 8 jumbo shrimp, shelled, deveined, and butterflied
> 1/2 teaspoon kosher salt
> 1/2 teaspoon cracked black peppercorns
> 1 large lime
> 2 sprigs fresh mint, for garnish
> 1 cup Meyer Lemon Date Relish (see page 146)

Drizzle the olive oil over the shrimp. Heat a heavy cast iron pan until it is very hot, about 5 minutes. Place the salt and pepper in the pan and cook for one minute. Add the shrimp and cook them quickly for approximately 1 minute on each side, until they turn a bright pink-red.

To serve, remove the shrimp from the pan and place on a platter. Squeeze the lime juice over them, garnish with mint, and serve immediately with Meyer Lemon Date Relish.

Shrimp Bigarrade *with a* Caribbean Ratatouille

For the distinctive sour and sweet flavor of these shrimps, I reached back into classic culinary history. While reading my treasured first edition of Escoffier, I came across his original recipe for Duck à la Orange, *or à la* Bigarrade. *The sauce in my recipe is made with bitter oranges in a similar technique. Unlike a traditional ratatouille, this version uses an array of garden vegetables from the Caribbean.*

➤ *Serves 4*

1 large sour orange, zested and juiced
1 bay leaf
2 sprigs fresh thyme
16 jumbo shrimp, cleaned, peeled, and deveined
3 tablespoons olive oil
3 large shallots, minced
2 tablespoons brown sugar
1 tablespoon champagne vinegar
1 1/2 cups freshly squeezed orange juice
1/2 teaspoon salt
1/2 teaspoon ground black pepper
2 tablespoons bias-cut scallions, for garnish

Caribbean Ratatouille

2 tablespoons olive oil
1 large onion, sliced
1 small green plantain, diced
1 cup diced calabaza, acorn squash, or pumpkin
2 medium chayotes, diced
2 medium Anaheim chiles, seeded and diced
1 red bell pepper, seeded and diced
1/2 tablespoon chopped garlic
1 teaspoon dried oregano
1 teaspoon ground cumin
1 teaspoon ground black peppercorns
1 tablespoon kosher salt
1 cup freshly squeezed orange juice

In a small pan of boiling water, cook the sour orange zest for one minute. Drain well. In a stainless steel bowl, combine the cooked zest, orange juice, bay leaf, thyme, and shrimp. Cover and marinate for about 1 hour.

While the shrimp are marinating, make the ratatouille. In a large Dutch oven, warm the olive oil. Add the onion and cook until translucent. Add each of the vegetables at 2-minute intervals, starting with the green plantain, calabaza, chayotes, Anaheim chiles, and red pepper. Stir well, being careful not to crush any of the vegetables.

Season with garlic, oregano, cumin, black pepper, and salt. Add the orange juice and simmer for 5 minutes, or until the vegetables are tender. Avoid overcooking, as the individual flavors of the vegetables will be lost.

To cook the shrimp, warm the olive oil in a large pan. Add the shallots and cook until translucent, approximately 2 minutes. Add the shrimp and marinade and sauté for approximately 1 minute over medium heat. Add the brown sugar and mix until dissolved. Add the champagne vinegar and stir together. Pour in the orange juice and bring the mixture to a simmer. Remove the shrimp to a covered dish in a warm oven. Continue to simmer the cooking liquid until reduced by half. Remove and discard the thyme and bay leaf and season the sauce with salt and pepper. Continue to cook the sauce until thickened.

To serve, arrange the shrimp on a warm service platter, pour the sauce around the shrimp, and garnish with scallions. Serve with the Caribbean Ratatouille.

Lobster Hash
with Citrus Sofrito Cruda

Hash is a casual dish that is meant to be fulfilling and comforting. Using lobster brings it to an entirely different—and luxurious—level.

➤ *Serves 4*

4 medium sweet potatoes
3 tablespoons olive oil
$1/2$ cup julienned shallots
2 teaspoons chopped garlic
$1/2$ teaspoon ground star anise
1 cup diced sweet red bell peppers
2 teaspoons diced serrano chile
2 cups cooked, diced Maine lobster meat
$1/4$ cup orange juice concentrate
2 tablespoons chopped flat leaf parsley
1 tablespoon kosher salt
1 cup Citrus Sofrito Cruda (see page 148)
8 sprigs fresh cilantro, for garnish

Preheat the oven to 350°. Wash and dry the sweet potatoes. Using a fork, pierce the skin several times to prevent them from bursting. Place them directly on the oven rack. Bake for 45 minutes, until they are slightly soft to the touch. Remove from the oven and let cool completely. Peel and dice into a small $1/2$-inch cubes.

In a large, flat griddle pan, warm the olive oil on medium heat. Add the shallots and cook until caramelized, approximately 3 to 4 minutes. Add the garlic and the diced sweet potato. Toss together and cook for 1 minute. Add the star anise, red peppers, serrano chile, lobster meat, orange juice concentrate, and parsley. Sauté together for another minute and season with salt.

To serve, arrange an oval mound of the hash in the center of each plate, spoon the Citrus Sofrito Cruda around the plate, and garnish with cilantro.

Pan-Roasted Scallops
with Mandarins, Cinnamon, and Chickpeas

The Middle Eastern influence is very clear in the contrasting textures and flavors incorporated in this easy-to-prepare recipe.

➤ *Serves 4*

4 large mandarins
1 pound bay scallops
$1/4$ teaspoon ground cinnamon
$1/2$ teaspoon ground allspice
3 tablespoons olive oil
$1/2$ teaspoon chopped garlic
1 cup cooked chickpeas
1 medium European cucumber, scooped out with a small melon baller
$1/2$ teaspoon kosher salt
$1/2$ teaspoon black peppercorns, ground

Peel and segment 2 of the mandarins, julienne 2 tablespoons of the peel, and juice the other 2 mandarins. In a large stainless steel bowl, combine the scallops, mandarin peel, cinnamon, allspice, and olive oil. Cover and refrigerate for 1 hour.

Heat a heavy-bottomed sauté pan. Once the pan is hot, add the scallops and sauté for 2 minutes. Add the garlic, chickpeas, mandarin juice, and cucumber, and season with salt and pepper. Add the mandarin segments and remove from the heat.

Sour Orange Game Hen
with Plantain Fritters

My first introduction to the homegrown sour orange was in Miami, where I first tasted Pollo con Mojo. *It was love and challenge at first bite. Now I love to use these same traditional sour orange flavors to add zing to game hen.*

➤ *Serves 4*

¹/₄ cup sour orange juice

¹/₄ cup soy sauce

¹/₄ cup honey

1 tablespoon chopped garlic

¹/₂ teaspoon ground allspice

¹/₂ teaspoon chopped fresh gingerroot

2 teaspoons kosher salt

1 teaspoon ground black pepper

3 tablespoons olive oil

4 (18 ounce) Rock Cornish game hens

2 quarts peanut oil

2 large very ripe plantains

Combine the sour orange, soy sauce, honey, garlic, allspice, ginger, salt, pepper, and olive oil. Rub the seasoning mixture on the hens and let them marinate for 1 hour at room temperature.

Preheat the oven to 425°. Set the birds on a roasting rack, breast up, and place in the center of the oven. Cook for 15 minutes. Reduce the heat to 350° and baste the birds. Continue roasting for 20 to 25 more minutes, basting regularly until the interior juices run clear. Remove from the oven and let them rest for 5 minutes.

Fill a deep fryer with the oil. Preheat the oil to 375°. Peel and cut the plantains in 2-inch chunks. Fry the plantains for about 5 minutes, until well caramelized. Turn them onto an absorbent paper towel to blot the excess oil and serve immediately.

Citrus Barbecue Short Ribs

Grapefruit, oranges, and lemons combine in a delicious marmalade-style barbecue glaze. The hot and spicy citrus and beef make an unusual and delicious combination—a welcome departure from the typical tomato-based barbecue sauce.

➤ *Serves 4*

4 pieces beef short ribs (approximately 12 ounces each)
1 medium carrot, chopped
1 large onion, chopped
1 stalk celery, chopped
1 tablespoon kosher salt
1 tablespoon whole black peppercorns
1 bay leaf
1 large lemon, quartered
1 tablespoon olive oil
1 teaspoon chopped garlic
$\frac{1}{2}$ teaspoon dried thyme
3 tablespoons Three-Citrus Barbecue Marmalade (see page 151)

Trim the excess fat from the short ribs. Fill a large pot with the ribs, carrot, onion, celery, salt, peppercorns, bay leaf, and lemon. Add enough water to cover completely. Over medium heat, bring to a boil. As the ribs cook, skim the white foam from the liquid's surface. Continue to simmer the ribs for 1 hour to 1 hour and 15 minutes, until the ribs start to become tender. Remove from the heat and let the ribs cool in the stock.

Preheat a grill. In a small bowl, combine the olive oil, garlic, and thyme. Brush the ribs with half the Three-Citrus Barbecue Marmalade, then begin grilling the meat. Grill for approximately 5 minutes on each side, until meat is thoroughly browned. Brush on the remaining marmalade, glazing each side, and continue to grill for another 3 to 4 minutes until all of the ribs are well glazed and caramelized.

Pommelo Pork Chops *with*
Toasted Cumin and Black Bean Hummus

This flavor profile reaches into Cuba for its historical roots, but quickly advances past the Caribbean borders to be a classic of New World cuisine. Its unique flavor comes from the citrus-infused peppercorns.

➤ *Serves 4*

1 lime
½ tablespoon peppercorns
2 large pommelos
1 tablespoon cumin seeds, toasted
1 tablespoon minced fresh rosemary
1 tablespoon chopped garlic
3 tablespoons olive oil
1 teaspoon kosher salt
4 (8-ounce) pork chops
2 cups Black Bean Hummus (see page150)

Wash the lime and let it come to room temperature. On a flat work surface, group the peppercorns together. Holding the lime in the palm of your hand, crush and roll the citrus over the peppercorns. Repeat several times until the citrus oils are released onto the peppercorns. Crack the peppercorns in a grinder or mortar and pestle and set aside.

Cut the pommelos in half and squeeze out as much juice and pulp as possible. Reserve the other half pommelo to be peeled and segmented for garnish.

In a small bowl, combine the cumin seeds, rosemary, garlic, citrus peppercorns, olive oil, salt, and pommelo juice. Coat the pork chops with the mixture. Marinate for 30 minutes. When you are ready to cook the chops, preheat a grill or broiler. (It's essential to cook this meat over very high heat to seal in the flavors and juices.) An important part of chop cooking is to mark or brand the chop with the cross hatching of the grill, which can be done very easily. Begin by grilling the chop on the first side for 2 minutes, then turn the chop 45 degrees and continue grilling the same side for another minute or so. Turn the chop over and grill the other side the same way. Remove the chops from the grill. Serve with Black Bean Hummus and pommelo segments.

Skirt Steak *with Zinfandel Mojo* *and Salsa Turned Orange*

The combination of orange and beef has its roots firmly planted in Asia. Since fresh fruit was not always available, dried orange zest was used to add a citrus aroma.

➤ *Serves 4*

2 tablespoons chopped dried orange zest
1 cup red Zinfandel
¼ cup honey
1 tablespoon minced gingerroot
1 tablespoon minced garlic
½ cup freshly squeezed orange juice
¼ cup freshly squeezed lime juice
1 teaspoon kosher salt
1 teaspoon ground black pepper
2 to 2½ pounds skirt steak
2 tablespoons olive oil
2 tablespoons chopped fresh cilantro leaves, for garnish
1 cup Salsa Turned Orange (see page 153)

To prepare the mojo, in a small saucepan bring the orange zest and wine to a simmer. Simmer approximately 5 minutes to reduce the liquid by half. Remove from the heat and add the honey, ginger, and garlic. Let cool for 10 minutes, then add the orange juice, lime juice, half the salt, and half the pepper. Let cool completely before use.

Place the steak in a shallow pan and season with the remaining salt and pepper. Pour the mojo over the steak. Cover and refrigerate for 1 hour.

Preheat a broiler or grill. Remove the steak from the marinade and drizzle with olive oil. Grill the steak for 2 to 3 minutes on each side, until medium rare. Remove the steak and let it rest for 3 minutes.

To serve, slice the meat on the bias against the grain. Garnish with cilantro and serve with Salsa Turned Orange.

Valencia Orange Creamsicle with Crisp Orange Stix

While I was growing up, I always looked forward to the arrival of the Good Humor Man and his three-wheel refrigerated bicycle cart. Now that I'm grown, I prefer this sophisticated version of my old favorite.

➤ *Serves 4*

4 large Valencia oranges
4 cups sugar
$1/2$ vanilla bean, split lengthwise

Crisp Orange Stix

2 cups sifted flour
$1/2$ teaspoon baking powder
$1/8$ teaspoon baking soda
$1/2$ teaspoon salt
$2/3$ cup shortening
3 tablespoons grated orange rind
$1/2$ cup brown sugar
$1/3$ cup sugar
1 large egg
2 tablespoons orange juice
1 quart vanilla bean ice cream

In a large pot with plenty of water, simmer the whole oranges for 1 hour, then drain and let cool. In the same pot, dissolve the sugar in four cups of water over medium heat. Slice a $1/2$-inch off the top of each orange. Then add the oranges, tops, and vanilla bean into the water. Simmer over low heat for $2^1/2$ hours. When the oranges are done, remove them from the heat and set aside to cool. Refrigerate overnight.

To make the stix, preheat the oven to 400°. Sift together the flour, baking powder, baking soda, and salt. Set aside.

In a large bowl, cream together the shortening, orange rind, and sugars using an electric mixer. Beat until the mixture is light and fluffy, approximately 3 to 4 minutes. Add the egg and orange juice and beat well. Gradually add the sifted dry mixture and blend thoroughly.

Using your hands, roll the dough into pencil-thin ropes. Cut each rope into 4-inch stix and place on a parchment-lined baking sheet. Bake for 6 to 8 minutes, until golden brown. Remove from oven and let cool.

To serve, remove the oranges from the syrup and spoon out any seeds, leaving the pulp inside. Fill each orange with ice cream, replace the top, and serve with syrup and Crisp Orange Stix.

Kumquat Cookies

I have fond memories of my first attempt at culinary entrepreneurship—selling lemonade on a street corner in Brooklyn, New York for 2 cents a glass! I only wish that I could have baked these easy cookies to go along with it.

➤ *Makes 6 dozen cookies*

6 tablespoons freshly squeezed lemon juice

1 cup water

2 cups sugar

12 large kumquats, sliced crosswise

1 cup butter

2 large eggs

3 cups sifted flour

1 teaspoon baking soda

sugar for sprinkling

In a small nonreactive saucepan, combine the lemon juice, water, and half of the sugar. Heat gently until the sugar dissolves and bring to a simmer. Add the sliced kumquats. Slowly simmer this syrup for 20 minutes, and remove it from the heat. Let cool. Drain and reserve liquid.

Preheat the oven to 350°. Using a small electric mixer, cream together the butter and the remaining sugar in a mixing bowl. Add the eggs one at a time, beating well after each addition. Combine the flour and baking soda, and stir into the butter mixture alternately with $1/2$ cup of the reserved syrup.

On a nonstick cookie sheet, drop teaspoon-sized rolled dough balls, 2 inches apart. Press a kumquat slice into the center of each cookie. Bake for approximately 7 minutes, or until the edges are lightly browned. Remove from the oven and brush the hot cookies lightly with the remaining syrup, then sprinkle with sugar.

Lemon Meringue Kisses
with Lemon Curd

Lemon meringue is a treat that doesn't have to wait for summer. Try these kisses on a cool afternoon.

➤ *Serves 6*

3 egg whites
1/4 teaspoon cream of tartar
Dash salt
1/2 cup sugar
1/2 teaspoon lemon extract
1 large lemon, thinly sliced (for garnish)

Lemon Curd
2 large lemons
3 egg yolks
1 cup sugar
1 tablespoon butter

In a very clean mixing bowl, beat together the egg whites, cream of tartar, and salt using an electric mixer. Beat until foamy. Gradually add sugar and beat on high until stiff and glossy. Fold in the lemon extract.

Preheat oven to 200°. Line a cookie sheet with parchment paper. With a pencil, draw 12 circles, each approximately 3 inches across. Spoon the mixture into the circles. Using the back of the spoon, round out the center of each meringue to form a cup. Bake for 1 hour or until the shells lift off the paper easily. Carefully remove the shells from the paper and cool on a wire rack.

To make the lemon curd, juice the lemons and grate the rinds finely. In the top of a double boiler, whisk the egg yolks and sugar until thickened and pale. Add the rind, juice, and butter. Continue whisking over high heat, stirring constantly until thickened and smooth.

Fill each shell with lemon curd and garnish each plate with fresh lemon slices.

Blood Orange Marmalade Soufflé with Chocolate Grand Marnier Sauce

This warm, sweet, luscious dessert contains no egg yolks or butter—but with its decadent flavor, you'll never guess.

➤ *Serves 4*

8 egg whites
$^1/_2$ cup sugar, plus extra sugar for soufflé molds
1 dash salt
$^3/_4$ cup Blood Orange Marmalade (see page 149)
$^1/_2$ teaspoon orange zest

Chocolate Grand Marnier Sauce

4 ounces bittersweet chocolate
1 ounce Grand Marnier
Powdered sugar, for garnish

Preheat the oven to 350°. Lightly spray 4 individual soufflé molds with a nonstick cooking spray and dust each with sugar. Using a clean copper bowl, whip the egg whites to a froth, then gradually add the sugar and salt. Beat until stiff and glossy, then fold in the Blood Orange Marmalade and orange zest. Turn mixture into the sugared soufflé molds. Bake for 20 minutes.

While soufflés are baking, chop the chocolate into small pieces. Melt the chocolate in a double boiler or in a microwave oven that is set on medium for approximately 30 to 35 seconds, being careful not to scorch the chocolate. Add the Grand Marnier to the melted chocolate and stir well.

Remove the soufflés from the oven. Dust with powdered sugar and serve immediately with the Chocolate Grand Marnier Sauce. You can also try some Shamouti Orange Biscotti (see next page) as an accompaniment.

Shamouti Orange Biscotti

Along with a glass of your favorite freshly brewed tea, this biscotti surely will warm your heart.

➤ *Makes 30 biscotti*

2 cups all-purpose flour

1 cup sugar

1 teaspoon baking soda

3 large eggs

$1/2$ teaspoon vanilla extract

3 tablespoons grated Shamouti orange zest

$2/3$ cup shelled, chopped pistachios

Preheat the oven to 300°. In a large mixing bowl, combine the flour, sugar, and baking soda. In a separate bowl, lightly beat the eggs with the vanilla and orange zest, and then add the mixture to the dry ingredients. Mix all this together well and add the pistachios.

On a well-floured surface, knead the dough for 2 to 3 minutes. Divide the dough in 2 pieces and shape each into a log about 2 inches wide. Place the logs on a parchment covered baking sheet. Bake the loaves for approximately 25 minutes until cooked through. Remove from the oven and let cool for about 5 minutes.

Cut into $3/4$-inch-thick slices. Place the slices on a cookie sheet and bake at 275° for another 45 minutes, until the biscotti are golden brown and dry. Remove from the oven and cool.

Chocolate Grapefruit Truffles

I like to call these delectable truffles grapefruit teasers. Each bite offers a startling, rich flavor.

➤ *Makes 25 to 30 pieces*

2 large grapefruits
2½ cups superfine sugar
5 ounces coating chocolate
½ cup cocoa powder

Using a vegetable peeler, peel the grapefruit skin from top to bottom in inch-wide strips. Take care to remove the white pith, which is quite bitter. Cut each strip cross-wise into diamonds measuring 1 inch by 1 inch.

In a small pot of boiling water, blanch the peels for approximately 4 to 5 minutes on a low simmer. Strain the peel and cool under cold running water. Repeat the process two more times, with fresh water each time. Then, in the same pot, dissolve the sugar in 2 cups of water by bringing it to a boil. Add the grapefruit peel and cook for 1½ hours on a very low simmer. Remove the peels and let them drain on a wire rack.

Melt the coating chocolate in a double boiler or a small bowl in the microwave for 30 to 35 seconds on medium. Mix well. Using a dipping fork, coat each piece of peel in the chocolate. Place on a wire rack to dry. Toss the truffles in the cocoa powder, generously coating both sides. Shake off excess cocoa and remove truffles to a clean plate.

Red Banana Brulée *with*
Clementine Fruit Salsa

*The red-skinned banana has a more aromatic
vanilla flavor than its cousin the yellow banana.
The salsa gets its special rich flavor from a tea and
citrus combination.*

➤ *Serves 6*

Clementine Fruit Salsa

3 large clementine mandarins

1 medium grapefruit

1 medium mango

2 tablespoons honey

3 tablespoons brewed orange pekoe tea

2 tablespoons toasted slivered almonds

Red Banana Brulée

6 medium ripe red bananas

1 tablespoon freshly squeezed lime juice

¼ teaspoon pure vanilla extract

3 tablespoons light brown sugar

4 sprigs fresh mint

To prepare the salsa, peel the clementines and the grapefruit. Cut between the membranes of the grapefruit to
remove the segments and seeds. Cut the citrus segments
in thirds and place them in a stainless steel bowl. Peel,
seed, and dice the mango and add to the bowl. Add the
honey, tea, and almonds. Mix well and chill.

Peel the bananas. The skin is just a little thicker than a
yellow banana, so take care not to break the bananas. Split
the bananas in half lengthwise and place them in a flat
glass dish, cut side up. Combine the lime juice and vanilla, then brush the bananas with the mixture. Generously
spoon the brown sugar on the bananas.

Preheat a broiler to 500°. Place the sugar-topped
bananas under the broiler for 2 to 3 minutes, until they
are well caramelized. Remove from the broiler and let
cool for 1 minute before removing from the pan.

In colorful small bowls, evenly divide the Clementine
Fruit Salsa. Place half of Red Banana Brulée in each bowl
and garnish with fresh mint.

Frozen Key Lime Pie

Key limes may make you pucker, but this frozen pie will make you smack your lips for more.

➤ *Serves 6*

1 cup finely ground graham cracker crumbs
3½ tablespoons melted butter
½ cup key lime juice
¼ oz. clear gelatine
4 large egg yolks
1 teaspoon grated key lime rind
¼ cup sugar
1 14-ounce can sweetened condensed milk
¼ teaspoon vanilla extract

In a small mixing bowl, combine the graham crumbs and 3 tablespoons of the butter. Lightly butter a pie tin with the remaining butter. Press the crust mixture into the tin evenly and refrigerate to chill.

In a small mixing bowl dissolve the gelatine in the lime juice. In a separate bowl, beat the egg yolks, rind, and sugar until thickened and tinted green. Stir in the condensed milk, lime juice mixture, rind, and vanilla. Continue to stir until the mixture thickens, approximately 2 to 3 minutes.

Pour the finished key lime mixture into the chilled graham crust and place in the freezer for approximately 2 to 3 hours, or until frozen.

Meyer Lemon Date Relish

Sweet Meyer lemons contrast well with the richness of sundried dates. This unique relish has wonderful flavors enhanced by the coriander seed and mint.

➤ *Makes 2 cups*

2 large Meyer lemons

1 cup water

1 tablespoon crushed coriander seed

$\frac{1}{2}$ cup pine nuts

2 tablespoons olive oil

$\frac{1}{2}$ pound pitted and diced Medjool dates

3 tablespoons diced red onion

1 tablespoon shredded fresh mint

Remove the rind from the lemons. Trim off the white pith, cut the rind into fine shreds, and simmer in water for 5 minutes. Drain and cool the rinds. Juice both lemons and reserve.

In a dry heavy pan, toast the coriander and pine nuts together over low heat, until the pine nuts are lightly browned. Add the drained lemon rinds, olive oil, and lemon juice, then continue to cook over low heat for 2 minutes.

In a stainless steel bowl, combine the dates and red onion. Pour the lemon mixture into the bowl and mix well. Let stand for 30 minutes and serve garnished with mint.

Calamondin-Green Mango Chutney

Chutneys are one of those misunderstood condiments, most often relegated to Indian foods. This one, easy to make, will alter your perception of what constitutes a chutney and will surely join your list of favorite condiments.

➤ *Makes 1 quart*

3 large green mangoes
2 large ripe mangoes
4 large Calamondins
3 tablespoons olive oil
1 medium Spanish onion, finely diced
1 tablespoon minced gingerroot
1 cup light brown sugar
$^1/_2$ teaspoon ground cayenne pepper
1 tablespoon ground cumin
1 teaspoon ground allspice
1 teaspoon kosher salt
$^1/_4$ cup white wine vinegar
1 cup dry white wine

Peel the mangoes and remove the pits. Cut into $^1/_2$-inch dice. Wash the Calamondins and dice, removing the seeds.

In a large heavy saucepan, warm the oil. Add the onion and cook over low heat until it begins to brown and caramelize. Add the ginger and brown sugar and continue to cook for 3 to 4 minutes. Add the cayenne, cumin, allspice, and salt. Mix well and add the vinegar, white wine, diced mango, and calamondin to the mixture. Continue to simmer for 20 to 25 minutes, until the chutney is sufficiently thickened. Remove from the heat and cool. Cover and refrigerate.

Citrus Sofrito Cruda

Sofritos, which are usually combinations of tomato, garlic, and chiles, add much to the cuisine of Puerto Rico and other Caribbean islands. This sofrito, based on citrus, has a lighter, more lingering flavor than is usual.

➤ *Makes 2 cups*

1 cup freshly squeezed orange juice
$1/2$ cup freshly squeezed lime juice
2 tablespoons freshly squeezed lemon juice
1 medium onion, minced
1 tablespoon red chile powder
1 tablespoon ground ancho chile powder
$1/4$ teaspoon crushed red pepper flakes
1 tablespoon extra virgin olive oil
2 tablespoons light brown sugar
1 teaspoon kosher salt
1 tablespoon chopped fresh cilantro
1 large orange, peeled, seeded, and diced
1 medium lime, peeled, seeded, and diced

In a stainless steel bowl, whisk together the orange juice, lime juice, lemon juice, onion, red chile powder, ancho chile, red pepper flakes, extra virgin olive oil, brown sugar, and salt. Add the cilantro, diced oranges, and diced limes. Cover and refrigerate for 1 hour before serving.

Spicy Tangerine Salsa

The honey Murcott tangerine is my favorite for this spicy salsa. The Murcott's tangy acid and high sugar content are heightened by the heat of the Scotch bonnet chile.

➤ *Makes 2 cups*

4 large tangerines, peeled, seeded, and diced
1 tablespoon hoisin sauce
1 tablespoon minced gingerroot
1 tablespoon chopped fresh cilantro
1 tablespoon minced green onion
1 tablespoon lime juice
1/2 tablespoon Scotch Bonnet, seeded, and chopped

In a stainless steel bowl combine all of the ingredients. Cover and refrigerate for 1 hour before use.

Blood Orange Marmalade

Blood oranges take on a crimson hue when simmered with sugar. This rich red preserve looks beautiful and tastes great on English muffins.

➤ *Makes 6 pints*

4 cups thinly sliced, seeded blood oranges
1 cup thinly sliced, seeded sour oranges
9 cups water
9 cups sugar

In a large pot, combine the oranges and water. Bring to a boil and cook rapidly for 20 minutes or until tender. Add the sugar and cook over low heat, stirring until the sugar dissolves. Boil rapidly to jelly stage (220° on a candy thermometer), or approximately 40 minutes (the bubbling will dissipate and the fruit will become opaque). Remove from heat, skim foam from the surface, and let cool for 5 minutes.

Stir to distribute the fruit throughout the syrup, pour into hot sterilized jars, and seal at once.

Black Bean Hummus

The orange oil used in this recipe is very simple to make and versatile. Almost any variety of orange can be used. But remember to rinse the skin well first under cold running water. Cut the rind with a paring knife, just deep enough to trim ½ inch vertical strips. Skin the entire orange in this fashion and place the rinds into a glass jar. Pour 2 cups of canola oil into the jar and cover. Leave at room temperature for at least 2 days. Keep covered until ready to use. The oil will stay good for 3 months.

➤ *Serves 6*

2 cups cooked black beans
1 cup cooked chickpeas
¼ cup tahini paste
1 teaspoon minced garlic
1 teaspoon kosher salt
½ teaspoon ground cumin
½ teaspoon cayenne pepper
1 tablespoon chopped fresh cilantro
½ cup freshly squeezed lemon juice
2 tablespoons orange oil
Freshly ground black pepper

Using a food processor fitted with a steel blade, purée the black beans, chickpeas, tahini paste, garlic, salt, cumin, cayenne, cilantro, and lemon juice together until smooth.

Spoon the hummus onto a large flat plate and spread it out with the back of the spoon. Drizzle a small pool of olive oil in the center and top with freshly ground black pepper.

Three-Citrus Barbecue Marmalade

The botanists have had their chance at cross-breeding and hybridizing citrus, with wonderful results. In this recipe, I crossbreed marmalade with barbecue sauce to create a great new hybrid.

➤ *Makes 1 quart*

2 large grapefruits
2 large oranges
2 large lemons
6 quarts water
5 pounds sugar
4 large serrano chiles, seeded and diced
1 teaspoon ground mustard seed
1 teaspoon ground cardamom seed
1 teaspoon ground allspice
1 teaspoon kosher salt
2 cups grapefruit juice

Two days before you want to use or preserve this glaze, wash the fruits well. Cut the grapefruits, oranges, and lemons into very thin slices and remove the seeds. Put the fruits in a mixing bowl with the water. Cover and let stand for 24 hours.

The next day, turn the fruits and water into a large pot and bring to a boil. Boil for 1 hour or until tender. Then remove from the heat, cover, and again let stand for 24 hours.

On the last day, uncover the pot and add the sugar. Put the pan on the stove top and start to warm slowly, stirring occasionally, until the sugar dissolves. Add the serrano chiles, mustard seed, cardamom seed, allspice, salt, and grapefruit juice. Boil the marmalade rapidly over high heat for 45 minutes. Remove from the heat and let stand for 5 minutes.

If you plan to preserve the glaze, stir to distribute the fruit throughout the syrup, pour into hot sterilized jars, and seal at once.

Yuca Mojo, Green Olives, and Shaddock Salad

This mojo is thickened by the yuca (cassava) starch, which gives it nice body and flavor. The bitterness of the green olives is complemented by the shaddock salad.

➤ *Serves 4*

1 pound peeled yuca
2 tablespoons kosher salt
1 small onion, diced
1 tablespoon chopped garlic
3 tablespoons olive oil
3 cups orange juice
3 tablespoons lime juice
3 tablespoons chopped fresh cilantro
1 large segmented shaddock
1 small red onion, finely julienned
1 teaspoon pink peppercorns
1 teaspoon dark rum
$^{1}/_{2}$ cup green olives

Cut the yuca into 3-inch segments. Place in a pot with plenty of cold water to cover and half the salt. Bring to boil over medium heat. Simmer the yuca for 45 minutes until cooked through. Remove from the heat and let the yuca sit in the water. When cooled, remove the yuca from the liquid and cut into quarters.

To prepare the mojo, combine the onion, garlic, olive oil, orange juice, and lime juice in a small saucepan. Warm gently and simmer for 10 minutes. Remove mojo from the heat and add 2 tablespoons of the cilantro.

To prepare the shaddock salad, combine the shaddock segments, red onion, the remaining salt, peppercorns, and rum.

Add the yuca to the mojo and warm together for 3 to 4 minutes, then add the olives. Turn the mixture into a serving bowl and top the yuca with the shaddock salad. Garnish with the remaining cilantro.

Salsa Turned Orange

This salsa turned orange has all the components I love about salsa, but then I add fresh orange and rind to give it a new twist.

➤ *Serves 4*

2 large navel oranges, peeled, sectioned, and diced

3 large yellow tomatoes, peeled, seeded, and diced

1 large sweet onion, finely diced

2 large jalapeños, seeded, ribbed, and diced

2 tablespoons freshly squeezed lime juice

2 teaspoons grated orange rind

2 tablespoons extra virgin olive oil

2 tablespoons chopped cilantro leaves

$1/2$ teaspoon kosher salt

In a small stainless steel bowl, combine all of the ingredients. Toss them well and let stand at room temperature for 30 minutes before use.

Citrus of the World

Variety	Origin	Harvest	Section	Page
African	Africa	Nov.-Dec.	Sour Orange	88
Argentine	Argentina	Dec.-Feb.	Sour Orange	88
Australian Finger Lime	Australia	May-August	Unusual Citrus	102
Baboon	Brazil	July-Oct.	Lemon	70
Bahianinha	Brazil	Nov.-Feb.	Sweet Orange	20
Bearss	Florida	Oct.-Jan.	Lemon	70
Berna	Spain	Oct.-May	Sweet Orange	20
Bigaradier Apepu	France	Jan.-March	Sour Orange	88
Bittersweet	Mediterranean	Dec.-Feb.	Sour Orange	90
Box Orange	Philippines	Jan.-April	Unusual Citrus	102
Buddha's Hand	China	Ever-bearing or fall	Citron	82
Burgundy	Florida	Nov.-July	Grapefruit	54
Calamondin	China	Nov.-April	Unusual Citrus	102
Cameron Highlands	Malaysia	Nov.-March	Lemon	70
Cara Cara	Venezuela	Oct.-Jan.	Sweet Orange	20
Chinotto	China	Dec.-March	Sour Orange	90
Citrangequat	Florida	Dec.-Sept.	Unusual Citrus	104
Citron	India	Ever-bearing or fall	Citron	82
Clementine	Algeria	Nov.-Jan.	Mandarin	36
Cleopatra	India	Oct.-Dec.	Mandarin	36
Dancy Tangerine	China	Dec.-Jan.	Mandarin	38
Diamante	Italy	Ever-bearing or fall	Citron	82
Dream Navel	Florida	Oct.-Jan.	Sweet Orange	22
Duncan	Florida	Dec.-May	Grapefruit	54
Dweet	California	April-May	Mandarin	38
Escondido	Nicaragua	July-Oct.	Lemon	72
Etrog	Israel	Ever-bearing or fall	Citron	84
Eustis	Florida	Nov.-July	Unusual Citrus	104
Fairchild	California	Dec.-March	Mandarin	38
Flying Dragon	Japan	Nov.-Jan.	Unusual Citrus	104
Foster	Florida	Nov.-March	Grapefruit	54
Fremont	California	Nov.-Jan.	Mandarin	40
Glen Navel	Florida	Oct.-Dec.	Sweet Orange	22
Gou Tou	China	Feb.-March	Sour Orange	90
Hamlin	Florida	Oct.-Jan.	Sweet Orange	22
Hirado Buntan	Japan	Nov.-Feb.	Pummelo	62
Honey	California	Jan.-March	Mandarin	40
Hong Kong	Japan	Jan.-March	Kumquat	96

Variety	Origin	Harvest	Section	Page
I Chang	China	Nov.-March	Unusual Citrus	106
Indian Sweet	India	Nov.-March	Lime	78
Jaffa	Israel	Dec.-April	Sweet Orange	24
Jincheng	China	Dec.-March	Sweet Orange	24
Kaffir Lime	Southeast Asia	Aug.-March	Unusual Citrus	106
Key Lime	Asia	Ever-bearing	Lime	78
Kona	Hawaii	March-June	Sweet Orange	24
Late Navel	Spain	Jan.-March	Sweet Orange	26
Lee	Florida	Nov.-Dec.	Mandarin	40
Lemonquat	Florida	Dec.-July	Unusual Citrus	106
Liang Ping Yau	China	Nov.-March	Pummelo	62
Lisbon	Portugal	Oct.-Aug.	Lemon	72
Long Fruit	Japan	Oct.-Jan.	Kumquat	96
Malayan	Malay	Dec.-March	Kumquat	96
Marsh	Florida	Nov.-May	Grapefruit	56
Meiwa	China	Nov.-Apr.	Kumquat	98
Meyer	China	Nov.-March	Lemon	72
Minneola	Florida	Dec.-April	Mandarin	42
Moro	Sicily/Italy	Dec.-Jan.	Sweet Orange	26
Moro Tarocco	Sicily	Dec.-Jan.	Sweet Orange	26
Murcott	Florida	Jan.-March	Mandarin	42
Nagami	China	Nov.-Apr.	Kumquat	98
Nasnaran	Java	Dec.-Jan.	Unusual Citrus	108
Natsumikan	Japan	April-May	Mandarin	44
New Guinea Lime	New Guinea	May-Aug.	Unusual Citrus	108
Nigerian Powder Flask	Nigeria	Jan.-March	Unusual Citrus	108
Nippon Orangequat	Japan	April-May	Unusual Citrus	108
Nocatee	Florida	Dec.-March	Mandarin	44
Orange Jasmine	India	Nov.-March	Unusual Citrus	110
Ortanique	Jamaica	March-June	Unusual Citrus	110
Page	Florida	Oct.-Feb.	Mandarin	44
Pandan Wangi	Japan	Nov.-March	Pummelo	62
Parson Brown	Florida	Oct.-Jan.	Sweet Orange	28
Pera	Brazil	March-May	Sweet Orange	28
Pink Pommelo	California	Dec.-Feb.	Pummelo	64
Ponkan	India	Dec.-Jan.	Mandarin	46
Procimequat	Florida	Nov.-July	Unusual Citrus	110
Rangpur	India	Ever-bearing	Unusual Citrus	112
Red Shaddock	Swaziland/Africa	Nov.-March	Pummelo	64
Rhode Red	Florida	March-June	Sweet Orange	28

Variety	Origin	Harvest	Section	Page
Rio Red	Texas	Nov.-May	Grapefruit	56
Roble	Spain	Oct.-March	Sweet Orange	30
Ruby Red	Texas	Nov.-May	Grapefruit	56
Sampson	Florida	Dec.-March	Mandarin	46
Sanguinelli	Spain	Feb.-April	Sweet Orange	30
Satsuma	Japan	Oct.-Nov.	Mandarin	46
Seville	Spain	Jan.-March	Sour Orange	92
Shamouti	Israel	Dec.-May	Sweet Orange	30
Siamese Sweet	Thailand	Nov.-March	Pummelo	64
Sinton	Texas	Dec.-March	Unusual Citrus	112
Star Ruby	Texas	Dec.-May	Grapefruit	58
Sunburst	Florida	Nov.-Dec.	Mandarin	48
Sydney Hybrid	Australia	July-Sept.	Unusual Citrus	112
Tahiti	Unknown	Jan.-Sept.	Lime	78
Temple	Jamaica	Jan.-March	Mandarin	48
Triumph	Florida	Nov.-April	Grapefruit	58
Tunis	Tunisia	Jan.-March	Sour Orange	92
Ugli	Jamaica	Oct.-April	Mandarin	50
Valencia	Spain/Portugal	March-June	Sweet Orange	32
Volkamer	Mediterranean	Oct.-March	Lemon	74
Wainwright	California	Dec.-Feb.	Pummelo	66
Washington Navel	California	Nov.-Feb.	Sweet Orange	32
Wekiwa	Florida	Nov.-Jan.	Mandarin	50
Willowleaf	China	Oct.-Dec.	Mandarin	50

BIBLIOGRAPHY

Batchelor, Leon Dexter; Walter Reuther; and Herbert John Webber (eds.). *The Citrus Industry*, rev. ed., Volume 1. Berkeley: University of California Press, 1967.

Hendrickson, Audra, and Jack Hendrickson. *Surprising Citrus: A Cookbook*. Pownal, Vermont: Garden Way Publishing, 1988.

Jackson, Larry K. *Citrus Growing in Florida*, 3d ed. Gainesville, Florida: University Presses of Florida, 1990.

Lawless, Julia. *The Illustrated Encyclopedia of Essential Oils*. Rockport, Mass: Element Books Inc., 1995.

McPhee, John. *Oranges*. New York: Farrar, Straus and Giroux, 1967.

Morton, Julia F. *Fruits of Warm Climates*. Miami: JF Morton Publishing, 1987.

Ray, Richard, and Lance Walheim. *Citrus*. Los Angeles: Price Stern Sloan, Inc., 1980.

Saunt, James. *Citrus Varieties of the World*. Norwich, England: Sinclair International, 1990.

Simeti, Mary Taylor. *Pomp and Sustenance: Twenty-Five Centuries of Sicilian Food*. New York: Henry Holt and Company, 1989.

Sinclair, Walter B. *The Biochemistry and Physiology of the Lemon and Other Citrus Fruits*. Oakland: ANR Publications, 1984.

Ward, Artemas. *The Grocer's Encyclopedia*. New York: James Kempter Printing Company, 1911.

Whiteside, J. O., et al., eds., *Compendium of Citrus Diseases*. Minneapolis-St. Paul: American Phytopathological Society, 1988.

Acknowledgments

A heartfelt thanks to a few special people who helped make this book possible.

To my growing family of Judi, Deanna, and Liza

For the staff at Chef Allen's Restaurant:

Doreen Moll, Tim Andriola, Dennis Lott, Kristin Lemmo, Tamara Page, Courtney Steward, and Dale LoSasso

For research and fruit harvesting:

Bob Crawford, Florida Department of Agriculture

Michael C. Kesinger, Florida Citrus Budwood Protection Program

Charles A. Thornhill, Plant Protection Specialist

Claire Peters, Sunkist Growers

Dr. Peggy Mauk, University of California, Riverside Coop Extension

William J. Wiltbank, University of Florida, Gainesville

Chris Rollins, Tropical Fruit and Spice Park

Maurice Kong, Rare Fruit Council

Norman Traner, Eco Farms

Michele Doto, Alex Produce

Christy Schielke and Tirsa Becerra, Carnival Fruit Company

For helping the book vision to become a reality:

Frank Flynn, Mariah Bear, Kirsty Melville, Phil Wood, Mayra Cardenas, and Heide Lange